BEST
WINES

THE IRISH TIMES

BEST WINES

MARY DOWEY

TOWN
HOUSE
DUBLIN

First published in 2001 by

TownHouse and CountryHouse
Trinity House
Charleston Road
Ranelagh
Dublin 6
Ireland

3 5 7 9 10 8 6 4 2

A CIP catalogue record for this book is available from the British Library.

ISBN: 1 86059 143 4

Cover design: Terry Foley
Typeset: Steven Hope Design
Printed in Finland by WS Bookwell

Contents

Acknowledgements

My first and biggest debt of thanks goes to *The Irish Times* for having the courage, six years ago, to entrust the wine column to a raw amateur enthusiast. I also want to thank the Irish wine trade for their support and patience in the face of constant nagging from a deadline-crazed correspondent. I am grateful to Treasa Coady and Claire Rourke of TownHouse and CountryHouse Publishers for all their encouragement and help with the shaping of this book. Finally, a big thank you to all the readers of the *Irish Times'* wine column. Your keen interest encourages me to keep pulling corks. I hope mine does the same for you.

Introduction

"What was that wine you wrote about a few weeks ago - that big red from southern Italy? I meant to cut the piece out of the paper, but of course I didn't." Readers of the *Irish Times'* wine column often stop me in the street, or email me to retrieve the details of particularly enticing bottles. I hope this book will be a handy reference to 250 of the most worthwhile wines I have recommended over the past few years. To me they represent the best of the best - wines that stand out from the crowd for flavour, interest and value.

Value is important, because the emphasis here is on everyday drinking. Almost all the wines cost under £25 and well over half cost under £10. Whatever the price, every single wine seems to me to be worth the money. If a lot of favourites are missing, it is simply because, delicious though they are, they currently cost a tad too much. Classed-growth Bordeaux, stellar Burgundies, benchmark Barolos, top vintage champagnes (and non-vintage glories like Krug), modern classics like Ridge, Cloudy Bay and the SuperTuscans. . .these and many other beauties have been bypassed in the hunt for wines with a more convincing price: quality ratio.

Unlike many buying guides, this one is arranged primarily according to wine colour and weight. These are the key considerations for wine shoppers, I believe. You think, "We're having a hearty beef casserole tonight - I need to buy a big strapping red." Rather than stopping to ponder the complexities of Shiraz versus Sangiovese or South Africa versus the south of France. Still, there is a clear demarcation in each section between Old World and New World wines, since people tend to veer towards one or the other. Country of origin comes next, and all the details about grape varieties are there if you need them.

The final selection, arrived at after many late, agonising nights, is broad - reflecting the thrilling diversity of the wine world today. The wines included come from 13 countries and represent 40 grape varieties (not counting another dozen esoteric bit players in blends.) Drawn from the lists of 44 importers of wine into Ireland - from the giants to one-man bands - I think they also show in microcosm the terrific vitality and variety that now make the Irish wine scene so exciting.

However, if the choice is wide in some ways, it is narrow in another. It's a personal selection, revealing all my own likes and dislikes - because, no matter how many objective criteria may be called into play when assessing a wine, it is as prone to the same subjective judgement in the end as music, literature or art. No two wine lovers have identical tastes. *Vive la différence!* My own preferences account for the strong line-up of white Burgundies (Chablis, especially), racy Rieslings and gutsy reds from the south of France and the south of Italy. Equally, tepid enthusiasm for certain wine styles and certain grapes shows up in thin coverage of such things as New World Chardonnay, Gewürztraminer and Pinotage.

The positive side of this naked bias is that all of the 250 wines featured are bottles I truly believe in - wines I am always happy to see. I retasted all of them in their current vintage while writing this book, and it was like meeting old friends again. I hope you will experience the same enjoyment. We're all lucky to love such an endlessly fascinating, civilising drink.

Mary Dowey
JULY 2001

About this Book

Sequence

In each chapter, countries are arranged alphabetically. Within each regional section, the wines are arranged according to price, starting with the least expensive.

Vintages

All the single vintages mentioned are available in Ireland at the time of going to press. Where two vintages are specified (e.g. 1999/2000), this indicates a crossover period, with a new vintage arriving before stocks of the previous one have been sold out. All the vintages of all the wines included in the book have been tasted.

Stockists

+   available in a few other outlets besides those listed
++   available in quite a number of other outlets
+++ available in many other outlets

Prices

The euro equivalents given are approximate, to accord with probable price points.

Bottle shapes

 Bordeaux shape: straight sides, high shoulders

 Burgundy or Rhone shape: wider with sloping shoulders

 Alsace or German shape: tall and slim

 Champagne shape: wide-bottomed and heavy

 Old-style fortified shape: straight neck, squat base

ALSACE

FRANCE

Dietrich Riesling Réserve
Alsace 1999

How many Alsace Rieslings have you come across at this price? This one may be less rich than the region's most famous examples, with their ample, spicy, petrolly character - but it's still a deliciously refreshing thirst quencher. Light and crisp as a Granny Smith, it ends up safely on the right side of tart. A great aperitif.

Grape Riesling
Alcohol 12%
Importer TDL
Stockists O'Briens · Foxs, Grafton St · McHughs, Kilbarrack · Mill Wine Cellar, Maynooth · O'Donovans, Cork ++

Price under £8 (under €10)

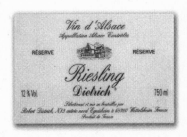

ALSACE

FRANCE

Hugel Alsace Pinot Blanc de Blancs
Cuvée Les Amours 1999

Look out for this wine all over the country, in restaurants that recognise how flexible Alsace Pinot Blanc is with a whole range of foods, including salads, vegetables, chicken, pork, Thai dishes. Quiet on the nose, it's super on the palate - a happy marriage of generous pear and apple fruit and zesty acidity.

Grape Pinot Blanc

Alcohol 12.5%

Importer Grants of Ireland

Stockists O'Briens · Vintry, Rathgar · Kielys, Mount Merrion · McHughs, Kilbarrack · Vineyard, Galway · Feeneys, Salthill ++

Price £9-£9.50 (€11.40-€12)

DISTRIBUTED IN IRELAND BY GRANTS OF IRELAND
ALSACE
APPELLATION ALSACE CONTRÔLÉE
DEPUIS 1639
CUVÉE LES AMOURS
·HUGEL·
PINOT BLANC DE BLANCS
MIS EN BOUTEILLE PAR HUGEL ET FILS · RIQUEWIHR · FRANCE

ALSACE

**Berrys' Own Selection Alsace Pinot Blanc
1999/2000**

It's all too easy to forget both Alsace and Pinot Blanc - a grape buried, in Ireland, under a million tonnes of Chardonnay. Put them together, in the hands of an organic producer like Domaine Mittnacht, and you get smoothness, freshness, honeyed fruit flavours, a long tangy finish . . . and, wonder of wonders, low alcohol. Versatile enough to go well with light food of all sorts - but I also love it all alone.

Grape Pinot Blanc
Alcohol 11.5%
Importer Berry Bros
Stockist Berry Bros, Harry St

Price about £10 (€12.70)

ALSACE

Trimbach Riesling, Cuvée Frédéric Emile
Alsace 1997

What you really need to do is buy Trimbach's flagship wine and store it away for years, so that it develops that rich, petrolly character that makes older Rieslings so intriguing. Although far too young to show the glorious complexity of which it's capable, this is already a superbly elegant wine, light to medium in body rather than an Alsace heavyweight.

Grape Riesling
Alcohol 13%
Importer Gilbeys
Stockists Sweeneys, Dorset St & Fairview · Vintry, Rathgar · McCabes, Blackrock & Foxrock · Jus de Vine, Portmarnock · Greenacres, Wexford ++

Price   £28–£29 (€35.50–€36.90)

BORDEAUX & THE SOUTHWEST

Domaine du Rey, Vin de Pays des Côtes de Gascogne 2000

Think of this as a deckchair special - a wine to sip in the garden when the sun in shining (or indoors when you need to conjure up instant summer). Drinking it is like diving head first into a fruit salad of apples, pears and melon with a sprig of mint for zest . . . Excellent value, and it's organic and Vegan Society-approved to boot.

Grapes Colombard, Gros Manseng, Ugni Blanc
Alcohol 11.5%
Importer J & T Davy
Stockists Searsons, Monkstown · Vintry, Rathgar · Murtaghs, Enniskerry · Pettitts in southeast · Karwig Wines, Carrigaline ++

Price about £7 (€8.90)

FRANCE

BORDEAUX & THE SOUTHWEST

FRANCE

Château Pique-Sègue
Montravel 2000

This old favourite from Bergerac could teach loftier Bordeaux, just up the road, a thing or two about endowing everyday wines with character and length. Carefully made from organically cultivated grapes, it has sweet gooseberry and greengage flavours cut by brisk and lingering acidity - and Semillon in the blend makes for good mouthfeel.

Grapes Sauvignon Blanc, Semillon, Muscadelle
Alcohol 12%
Importer Comans
Stockists selected SuperValus · Jus de Vine, Portmarnock · Sweeneys, Dorset St · Deveneys, Dundrum · Egans, Drogheda ++

Price about £7 (€8.90)

BORDEAUX & THE SOUTHWEST

Château Bertinerie
Premières Côtes de Blaye 2000

Eric Bantegnies, who makes this wine, is a dedicated experi-
menter in one of the areas of Bordeaux where great strides are
being made in the quality/value stakes. Fragrant and brilliantly
fresh, it has more ripeness and roundness than many a
Sauvignon-based French white. Equally tempting with food or
without.

Grape Sauvignon Blanc, Semillon, Muscadelle
Alcohol 12.5%
Importer Wines Direct
Stockist Wines Direct

Price under £8 (under €10)

FRANCE

BURGUNDY

Mâcon-Villages
Pierre Ponnelle 1999

This is nothing short of a miracle wine - one that offers the true character of white Burgundy at a bargain price. That's a fairly alien concept these days. Behind typical aromas of apples, pears and wet stones lies a smooth-textured Mâcon with ripe fruit yielding to a crisp, juicy finish. Four-star value.

Grape Chardonnay
Alcohol 13%
Importer Dunnes Stores
Stockists Dunnes Stores leading outlets

Price about £7 (€8.90)

BURGUNDY

**Marks & Spencer Chablis
1998**

Well made by the excellent La Chablisienne co-op (their Les Domaines Chablis Vieilles Vignes is on page 12), this is a tempting supermarket Chablis at very fair price. The fact that it's a little more mature than many is a bonus: honey-streaked apple flavours come through in a smooth, well-integrated wine with the lingering tang of classic Chablis.

Grape Chardonnay
Alcohol 12.5%
Importer Marks & Spencer
Stockist Marks & Spencer

Price about £9 (€11.50)

BURGUNDY

FRANCE

Chablis
Claude Paternot 1998

Here's another modestly priced Chablis that doesn't fall into the usual cheapie trap of being bitter and dilute - quite the opposite. With seductively ripe, appley fruit and a luxurious texture, it feels almost rich at first; then mineral and citrus tones kick in, leading to a long, firm finish. Exceptional at the price.

Grape Chardonnay
Alcohol 12.5%
Importer irelandonwine.com
Stockist irelandonwine.com

Price £9-£10 (€11.50-€12.70)

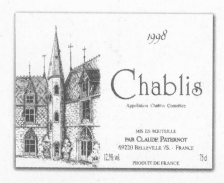

1998

Chablis

Appellation Chablis Contrôlée

MIS EN BOUTEILLE
PAR CLAUDE PATERNOT
69220 BELLEVILLE /S. · FRANCE
12.5% vol.   75 cl
PRODUIT DE FRANCE

BURGUNDY

**Baron de la Charrière Bourgogne
Cuvée Saint Vincent 1998**

A humble Bourgogne rather than one of your fancy appellations, but this brilliantly balanced, flavour-packed white from
Santenay superstar Vincent Girardin leaves a heap of bottles
from higher up the ranks for dead. White Burgundy as it should
be - suave, intense and alluring.

Grape Chardonnay
Alcohol 13%
Importer Oddbins
Stockist Oddbins

Price about £12 (€15.25)

FRANCE

FRANCE

BURGUNDY

Les Domaines Chablis Les Vieilles Vignes La Chablisienne 1996

Older vines yield smaller grapes with more concentrated flavours. This Chablis certainly supports the theory with an intense palate of ripe apples and peaches giving way to a honeyed finish which is still very fresh. In my experience, examples of straight Chablis from the admirable La Chablisienne co-op are more impressive than the *premier cru* and *grand cru* wines.

Grape Chardonnay
Alcohol 12.5%
Importer Mackenway
Stockists Terroirs, Donnybrook · Mortons, Ranelagh · Lord Mayor's, Swords · Londis, Malahide · Jus de Vine, Portmarnock · Ryan Vine, Navan +

Price about £13 (€16.50)

BURGUNDY

Chablis Saint Martin
Domaine Laroche 1999

Suppose you want a name that spells reliability and respectability? Although his company is now the biggest family-owned concern in Chablis, Michel Laroche has steered it beyond its 150th birthday with the rigour of a small-scale perfectionist. This unwavering example of classic Chablis has ripe fruit with a smidgeon of honey, lemon freshness and a good, steely finish.

Grape Chardonnay
Alcohol 12.5%
Importer Allied Drinks
Stockists Bennetts, Howth · Londis, Malahide · Higgins, Clonskeagh · Mill Wine Cellar, Maynooth · Old Stand, Mullingar · Galvins, Cork ++

Price about £14 (€17.75)

BURGUNDY

FRANCE

Chablis Premier Cru Montmains
Domaine de Chaude Ecuelle 1999

Not all *premier cru* Chablis are worthy of the name, by a long way, but this swish example really stands out. With ripe, almost mouth-filling fruit and stony mineral undertones, it has all the extra weight and persistence of flavour you could wish for, without sacrificing classic Chablis freshness. Well worth the price.

Grape Chardonnay
Alcohol 12.5%
Importer J S Woods
Stockists Jus de Vine, Portmarnock · Cheers-Gibneys, Malahide · DeVine Wine Shop, Castleknock · Michael's Wines, Mount Merrion · Wicklow Wine Co. · Cana Wines, Mullingar +

Price about £17.50 (€22.50)

LOIRE

FRANCE

Château du Cléray Muscadet Sèvre et Maine sur Lie 2000

Poor old Muscadet has been down on its luck these past few years - a forgotten fashion victim. Most are thin, miserable creatures that deserve their fate, but this one has enduring appeal, combining classic, spritzy freshness with a very smooth texture. Vital accompaniments: oysters and an ice bucket.

Grape Melon de Bourgogne
Alcohol 12%
Importer James Adams
Stockists selected SuperValus · selected Centras · Roches Stores · Superquinn · Molloys · Ardkeen, Waterford · Wine Centre, Kilkenny · Vineyard, Galway ++

Price £7-£8 (€8.90-€10)

LOIRE

FRANCE

Menetou-Salon Morogues
Domaine Henry Pellé 2000

I'd much prefer to drink this deliciously grassy, bracing Loire
Sauvignon than many of the bitter travesties emanating from
the grander appellation of Sancerre just a few miles further
east. Try it in summer with a goat's cheese salad and you will
have entered heaven.

Grape Sauvignon Blanc
Alcohol 12.5%
Importer Findlater
Stockists Kellys, Clontarf · Sweeneys, Dorset St & Fairview ·
Cheers-Gibneys, Malahide · On the Grapevine, Dalkey ·
Copes, Athy · O'Donovans, Cork +

Price £11-£12 (€13.90-€15.25)

LOIRE

Domaine Vacheron Sancerre
1999/2000

Like Chablis and Châteauneuf-du-Pape, Sancerre is a high-profile region, awash with indifferent wines at unjustifiably high prices, so you have to sift carefully to find quality. Although pricey, this perennial dinner-party favourite always seems to deliver. It has both the nettley, appley freshness and a smidgen of the flintiness of benchmark Sancerre, without being lean or mean.

Grape Sauvignon Blanc
Alcohol 12.5%
Importer Fèbvre
Stockists selected Superquinns · Molloys · Redmonds, Ranelagh · Thomas's, Foxrock · Cuisine de Vendange, Naas · Wine Centre, Kilkenny +

Price about £17 (€21.50)

FRANCE

FRANCE

LOIRE

Château de Tracy Pouilly-Fumé
2000

There's an intriguing hint of the minerally, almost smoky quality which distinguishes good Pouilly-Fumé from Sancerre and Menetou-Salon here - but there's also lovely gooseberry and green-apple intensity. This well-made wine is a can't-go-wrong restaurant and dinner-party stalwart.

Grape Sauvignon Blanc
Alcohol 13%
Importer Fèbvre
Stockists Thomas's, Foxrock · Cuisine de Vendange, Naas · Wine Centre, Kilkenny · Hartes, Clonakilty   +

Price about £18 (€22.90)

SOUTH

Domaine Bégude Chardonnay
Vin de Pays d'Oc, Comte Cathare 1999/2000

A simple but attractively fresh and creamy Chardonnay at a great price. Fastidious English winemaker Bertie Eden uses bio-dynamic methods to produce the wines under the Comte Cathare umbrella (see also page 143). Sceptics, eat (or drink) your heart out: all have wonderfully pure and vibrant flavours. In a world flooded with confected Chardonnays, that's a big plus.

Grape Chardonnay
Alcohol 13%
Importer Oddbins
Stockist Oddbins

Price about £7 (€8.90)

FRANCE

FRANCE

SOUTH

**Bergerie de l'Hortus Classique
Vin de Pays du Val de Montferrand 2000**

Delicately fruity and zippily fresh yet quite mouthfilling at the same time, this aromatic wine is a really well-balanced blend from clever Midi winemaker Jean Orliac (see pages 85 and 101). Viognier provides a touch of peachiness while Sauvignon Blanc delivers a lift and a refreshing tang in the finish. Summery and stylish.

Grapes Viognier, Chardonnay, Sauvignon Blanc
Alcohol 12.5%
Importer Wines Direct
Stockist Wines Direct

Price about £8.50 (€10.75)

Produit de France

2000

Rosé de Saignée

BERGERIE de L'HORTUS

....

PIC SAINT LOUP
Coteaux du Languedoc,
Appellation Coteaux du Languedoc Contrôlée

Mis en bouteille à France - 34270 par Jean Orliac
750 ml   Domaine de l'Hortus - 34270 Valflaunes   12.5 % alc. / vol.

GERMANY

Vier Jahreszeiten Dürkheimer Schenkenböhl Spätburgunder Weißherbst, Pfalz 1999

It's quite a shock to discover that this light, peachily fragrant white wine is made from the red grape, Pinot Noir. It's a lovely, light-hearted drink - the sort of thing you can just plunge into and enjoy. The name is the only problem. Look for the label's splashy butterfly.

Grape Spätburgunder (Pinot Noir)
Alcohol 12%
Importer Karwig Wines
Stockists Karwig Wines, Carrigaline · Molloys

Price about £9 (€11.50)

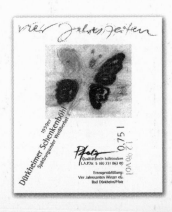

GERMANY

Dr L Riesling
Mosel-Saar-Ruwer, Loosen Bros 1999

Energetic Ernie Loosen in the Mosel is famous for his determi-
nation to demonstrate just how dazzling good German Riesling
can be. This may be his simplest wine, but it's both exhilarating
and exquisite. Hints of summer blossom, apples and honey are
shot through with mouth-watering acidity. You'll want to drink
lots, and, with an alcohol level of just 8.5%, you can.

Grape Riesling
Alcohol 8.5%
Importer James Nicholson
Stockists James Nicholson Direct · Raheny Wine Cellar ·
McHughs, Kilbarrack · Ryan Vine, Navan · Egans, Drogheda ·
Wine Centre, Kilkenny +

Price £9.50-£10 (€12-€12.70)

**D'Istinto Catarratto-Chardonnay
Sicilia 1999**

What emerges when the Australian giant BRL Hardy applies New World wine-making techniques to sunny Sicily's ripe grapes? A wildly drinkable wine with delicate echoes of peaches and lemon. Unlike most Italian whites, which only shine with food, this smooth, creamy middleweight is also fine on its own. Its red running-mate features on page 105.

Grapes Catarratto, Chardonnay
Alcohol 12.5%
Importer Allied Drinks
Stockists selected SuperValus · selected Centras · Roches Stores · Pettitts in southeast +++

Price about £6 (€7.60)

ITALY

Campogrande Orvieto Classico
Antinori 2000

Like Soave, Orvieto can be a tart, neutral nonentity - but Antinori's version is tasty enough to make you yearn for a big platter of parma ham (and another glass). Pleasantly fruity and mouth-wateringly refreshing, it's the perfect appetite-whetter for antipasti and summer salads.

Grapes Procanico, Grechetto, Verdello
Alcohol 12.5%
Importer Grants of Ireland
Stockists widely available

Price about £7 (€8.90)

**Lugana San Benedetto
Zenato 2000**

ITALY

There's a yeasty tang to good Lugana that really sets the taste-buds tingling - making it a terrific summer-food wine. This one from go-ahead maker Zenato (more of whose wines are on pages 163 and 167) combines a freshness that's almost spritzy with the lingering flavour of ripe apples.

Grape Trebbiano di Lugana
Alcohol 12%
Importer J & T Davy
Stockists Searsons, Monkstown · Layden Fine Wines, Liffey St ·
Michael's Wines, Mount Merrion · Ryan Vine, Navan ·
McGrorys, Donegal ++

Price about £9 (€11.50)

ITALY

Villa Canlungo Corno Rosazzo Pinot Grigio
Friuli, Collavini 2000

Everybody has everyday favourites. This is definitely one of mine. Zestily fruity (think of peaches, pears and a squeeze of lemon) with a subtle hint of herbs, it's all too easy to knock back as an aperitif - but is also wonderfully user-friendly with dishes dominated by vegetables and herbs: pizzas, pasta and salads.

Grapes Pinot Grigio
Alcohol 12.5%
Importer Woodford Bourne
Stockists Superquinn · SuperValus · Centras · Roches Stores · O'Briens · Fine Wines, Limerick · O'Donovans, Cork +++

Price £9-£10 (€11.50-€12.70)

I Frati Lugana, Cà dei Frati
1999/2000

From the Dal Cero family, rated among Lugana's most reliable
producers, comes this ultra-stylish version with real character
and depth. Alluring aromas of almonds and peaches are supported on the palate by persistent, creamy freshness. Throw an
Italian dinner party with this as the first wine.

Grapes Trebbiano di Lugana
Alcohol 12.5%
Importer Findlater
Stockists selected Superquinns · Raheny Wine Cellar · Kellys,
Clontarf · Cheers-Gibneys, Malahide · Mortons, Ranelagh ++

Price about £10 (€12.70)

ITALY

San Vincenzo Soave Classico
Anselmi 2000

Poor Soave suffers from an image problem, since so many of the nasties sold under its name ruin the reputation of the good stuff. This benchmark wine should convert the doubtful in a single glass. So much flavour! So much freshness! Roberto Anselmi leaves it on its lees for six months, so it has a lovely creamy, yeasty dimension - and oak gets nowhere near it.

Grapes Garganega, Chardonnay, Trebbiano di Soave
Alcohol 12.5%
Importer James Nicholson
Stockist James Nicholson Direct · Duffys, Terenure · Michael's Wines, Mount Merrion · Murtaghs, Enniskerry · Mill Wine Cellar, Maynooth · Le Caveau, Kilkenny +

Price £10-£10.50 (€12.70-€13.50)

Con Class Selección Especial
Rueda 2000

Although this zingy, fruity white always makes me think summer thoughts of flowering hedgerows and cut grass, it's actually a multi-purpose wine with year-round appeal. A runaway success in Ireland over the past few years, it demonstrates how deft the region of Rueda now is at producing fresh, lively whites.

Grapes Verdejo, Viura, Sauvignon Blanc
Alcohol 12.5%
Importer J & T Davy
Stockists Searsons, Monkstown · Mitchells, Kildare St & Glasthule · DeVine Wine Shop, Castleknock · Wicklow Wine Co. · Wine Centre, Kilkenny · Egans, Drogheda ++

Price £7.50-£8 (€9.50-€10.20)

SPAIN

Marqués de Riscal Sauvignon
Rueda 2000

Riscal was one of the first Spanish producers to make waves with fresher, fruiter white wines, focusing on Rueda rather than Rioja and recognising the value of Sauvignon Blanc for zip. This one has the gooseberry and herbaceous tones that have made New Zealand Sauvignon so popular - with maybe a little extra European crispness.

Grape Sauvignon Blanc
Alcohol 12.5%
Importer Findlater
Stockists selected SuperValus · selected Centras · Roches Stores · Molloys · O'Briens · Superquinn · Kellys, Artane · Londis Malahide ++

Price £7.50-£8 (€9.50-€10.20)

Martin Códax Albariño
Rías Baixas 2000

Spain's most fashionable white wine these days is Albariño, from Galicia in the north. Try this lively, unoaked version and you'll understand why. Smelling like a hedgerow full of flowers, tasting like fresh peaches with a big squeeze of lemon, it's superbly individual, smooth-textured and addictive.

Grape Albariño
Alcohol 12%
Importer Approach Trade Ireland
Stockists On the Grapevine, Dalkey · Layden Fine Wines, Liffey St · Egans, Liscannor · McCambridges, Galway · Karwig Wines, Carrigaline +

Price £11-£12 (€13.95-€15.25)

SPAIN

AUSTRALIA

Owen's Estate Sauvignon Blanc-Semillon
South Eastern Australia, Geoff Merrill 2000

From the stable of well-known mustachioed Aussie winemaker Geoff Merrill (his star red is on page 197), this smooth-textured blend combines sun-kissed fruit flavours - pineapple, sweet grapefruit, melon - with crisp acidity. Although it feels round and ripe, it's relatively low in alcohol. A wine to guzzle! Particularly delicious with Thai, Indian or fusion food, and great value.

Grapes Sauvignon Blanc, Semillon
Alcohol 12%
Importer Comans
Stockists all Cheers-Take Home outlets · Next Door outlets · Pettitts in the southeast · O'Donovans, Cork

Price £6-£6.50 (€7.60-€8.25)

**Wolf Blass White Label Semillon-Sauvignon Blanc
South Australia 2000**

Wolf Blass isn't synonymous with subtlety, either in person or
in the bottle - but here's a zesty, citrussy wine, so light-footed
in spite of its tropical fruit tones that you might almost take it
for a young Australian Riesling. One to tuck in the fridge when
the sun appears.

Grapes Semillon, Sauvignon Blanc
Alcohol 11.5%
Importer Edward Dillon
Stockists very widely available

Price £8-£8.50 (€10-€10.80)

Wynns Coonawarra Estate Riesling
1999/2000

Coonawarra, the great Cabernet zone, has no claim to Riesling fame ... except, perhaps, for this fruity number. Not a benchmark Aussie Riesling, maybe; just a really pleasant, easy drink, with generous fruit and all the reviving, lime-tinged freshness you could hope for.

Grape Riesling
Alcohol 12%
Importer Findlater
Stockists Vintry, Rathgar · Higgins, Clonskeagh · Cheers-Wicklow Arms, Delgany · Noble Rot, Navan · Vineyard, Galway ++

Price about £8.50 (€10.80)

**Wakefield Clare Riesling
Clare Valley 2000**

My favourite Riesling vintage from Wakefield so far. Although its flowery aromas are delicate, this wine really opens up on the palate, revealing pineapple and lime fruit with terrifically zippy acidity. Maybe the screwcap does the trick (as so many Australian Riesling makers now claim)? If you're feeling experimental, tuck a couple of bottles away. Even a modest Clare Riesling like this one will develop wonderfully over a decade.

Grape Riesling
Alcohol 13%
Importer Koala Wines
Stockists Superquinn · selected SuperValus · selected Centras · Roches Stores · Pettitts ++

Price £8-£9 (€10.20-€11.50)

AUSTRALIA

AUSTRALIA

Pewsey Vale Eden Valley Riesling 1999

Since the delicious Heggies isn't around any more (what madness!), this alternative from the Yalumba stable is probably Ireland's most refined Aussie Riesling at around a tenner. Delicate reminders of summer flowers, pears and mineral firmness fuse in a wine with a sherbet tingle and a long lime-and-honey finish.

Grape Riesling
Alcohol 12.5%
Importer Cassidy
Stockists McCabes, Blackrock & Foxrock · Kellys, Clontarf · Bourkes, Cabinteely · Wicklow Wine Co. · Greenacres, Wexford · O'Donovans, Cork +

Price about £10 (¤12.70)

Capel Vale Sauvignon Blanc-Semillon
Western Australia 2000

Australia doesn't often manage to do anything memorable with Sauvignon, but this smart blend from cool Western Australia is a shining exception. Almost European in character, it's light and delightfully zesty, with grassy, summery notes padded out by Semillon's creamy smoothness. Great length, great style.

Grapes Sauvignon Blanc, Semillon
Alcohol 12%
Importer Cassidy
Stockists Bennetts, Howth · McCabes, Blackrock & Foxrock · Bourkes, Cabinteely · Murtaghs, Enniskerry · Ardkeen, Waterford · Wine Centre, Kilkenny +

Price about £11.50 (€14.60)

AUSTRALIA

AUSTRALIA

Mount Langhi Ghiran Riesling
Victoria 1999

Amid a sea of sensational Rieslings sampled at the 2001 Australia Day tastings in London, this beauty really stood out. It's a memorable mouthful of pure, intense fruit with a mineral underpinning, nervy acidity and glorious spicy length. If this doesn't make you a Riesling fan on the spot, nothing will.

Grape Riesling
Alcohol 13.5%
Importer irelandonwine.com
Stockist irelandonwine.com

Price about £12.50 (×15.90)

1999

Riesling

PRODUCE OF AUSTRALIA

San Pedro Sauvignon Blanc
Molina 2000

Ex-Bordeaux flying winemaker Jacques Lurton is widely credited for the major leap forward at Viña San Pedro, a vast but quality-oriented Chilean enterprise. Look out for the San Pedro label in Dunnes Stores and the parallel Castillo de Molina label in restaurants. I especially like the Sauvignon - a lively mouthful of ripe gooseberries and passion fruit with surprisingly good length.

Grape Sauvignon Blanc
Alcohol 12.5%
Importer Dunnes Stores
Stockist Dunnes Stores

Price £6-£6.50 (€7.60-€8.25)

CHILE

Santa Ines Sauvignon Blanc
Maipo Valley 2000/2001

Here's another blameless Chilean Sauvignon Blanc - this time from a much smaller, family-owned winery. The recipe is the one we know and love: ripe gooseberry and tropical flavours with herbaceous freshness and a zesty, citrussy overlay. Nothing fancy - but no false notes either. Santa Ines Cabernet Sauvignon is featured on page 203.

Grape Sauvignon Blanc
Alcohol 13.5%
Importer Mackenway
Stockists Molloys · selected Cheers Take-Home outlets · Mortons, Ranelagh · Listons, Camden St · Brackens, Glasnevin · C&T, Skerries ++

Price about £7 (€8.90)

Carmen Reserve Sauvignon Blanc
Casablanca 2000/2001

If you feel like trading up a little, try this consistently delicious reserve Sauvignon from Carmen, a winery notable for the unfailing evenness of its performance (see also page 204). More intense in flavour than the basic version, it combines smooth, relatively subtle tropical fruit with enticing herbal notes and lingering crispness.

Grape Sauvignon Blanc
Alcohol 13%
Importer Edward Dillon
Stockists Superquinn and many good, independent off-licences

Price about £10 (€12.70)

CHILE

Château Los Boldos Sauvignon Blanc Vieilles Vignes Requinoa 2000

Laden with lime, lemon and grapefruit flavours and herbaceous freshness, this impressive Sauvignon is less sweet than many of its Chilean rivals. Made from organically cultivated, 64-year-old vines on an estate owned by the Massenez family, Alsace producers of eaux de vie, it's a sassy New World white with European restraint and remarkable length.

Grape Sauvignon Blanc
Alcohol 13.5%
Importer O'Briens
Stockist O'Briens

Price about £10 (€12.70)

NEW ZEALAND

Stoneleigh Vineyards Marlborough Sauvignon Blanc 2000

New Zealand has slipped in my affections of late; so many of the wines seem confected and cloying. Here's my everyday NZ favourite, though - a Sauvignon with lovely, soft, tropical fruit, a refreshing tang and quite decent length. It may lack the in-your-face aromas that are typically Kiwi, but at least it's balanced.

Grape Sauvignon Blanc
Alcohol 13.5%
Importer Irish Distillers
Stockists McCabes, Blackrock & Foxrock · Molloys ·Vintry, Rathgar · Mill Wine Cellar, Maynooth · Greenacres, Wexford · O'Donovans, Cork ++

Price about £8.50 (€10.80)

NEW ZEALAND

Hunter's Marlborough Sauvignon Blanc
2000

The real thing - classic Marlborough Sauvignon Blanc, with pungent aromas of nettles, blackcurrant leaves and gooseberries giving way to an explosion of parallel flavours that gently reverberate. Finely tuned and strikingly consistent, this truly appetising wine never becomes wearisome.

Grape Sauvignon Blanc
Alcohol 13%
Importer Gilbeys
Stockists Superquinn and many independent off-licences

Price £13-£14 (€16.50-€17.80)

Danie de Wet Chardonnay sur Lie
Robertson 2000

Rarely does a New World Chardonnay fill me with glee (although there are a few under Richer Whites). This budget-priced, unwooded example from a South African wine giant is just too delicious to bypass, however. Fruity at first (melons? apples?), it has yeasty freshness and a long, creamy aftertaste thanks to maturation on the yeast lees.

Grape Chardonnay
Alcohol 13%
Importer Oddbins
Stockist Oddbins

Price about £6 (€7.60)

Villiera Blue Ridge Blanc
Chenin Blanc-Sauvignon Blanc, Paarl 2000

Although consistency still seems to be a problem for South Africa, Villiera is a steady performer across the board. This blend makes for delicious summer drinking - like plunging into a pear and pineapple fruit salad, with a dash of lemon juice for freshness. It also proves that SA wines can be temptingly priced without tasting dull.

Grapes Chenin Blanc, Sauvignon Blanc
Alcohol 13%
Importer Grants of Ireland
Stockists selected Superquinns · selected SuperValus · selected Centras · Roches Stores · O'Briens · Martin's, Fairview · Joyces, Knocknacarra ++

Price about £7 (€8.90)

AUSTRIA

**Grüner Veltliner Smaragd,
Freie Weingärtner Wachau 1998**

An amazing mouthful - and I don't just mean that tortuous
name. Unctuous flavours of peaches, apricots and honey are
countered by lively lemon acidity in this glorious Viognier-like
Austrian white. Decadent, almost! It's the perfect smart aperitif
- or try it with scallops or crab and swoon.

Grape Grüner Veltliner
Alcohol 13.5%
Importer J & T Davy
Stockists Searsons, Monkstown · On the Grapevine, Dalkey ·
Ryan Vine, Navan · Wicklow Wine Co. · irelandonwine.com +

Price about £10 (€12.70)

ALSACE

Trimbach Pinot Gris Réserve
Alsace 1998

Alsace is always worth bearing in mind when you're on the trail of body and richness without recourse to new oak. This top-notch Pinot Gris has beautifully concentrated fruit flavours with hints of spice and nuts. Mouth-filling and distinctive, it is terrific with onion tart (just pretend you're in Alsace) but also good with pork and spicy dishes.

Grape Pinot Gris
Alcohol 13%
Importer Gilbeys
Stockists Tesco · selected Superquinns · Molloys · Sweeneys, Dorset St · Mill Wine Cellar, Maynooth · Greenacres, Wexford
++

Price £11-£12 (€13.95-€15.25)

ALSACE

Trimbach Gewürztraminer
Alsace 1998

Time for a confession. Gewürztraminer is a love-it-or-hate-it grape, and I'm afraid I veer towards antipathy for its upfront nature - the way it tends to scream lychees/rose petals/lime marmalade. This one is so well balanced, though, that I'm almost prepared to forgive it. And those big flavours, which include a touch of ginger, can go well with Chinese food.

Grape Gewürztraminer
Alcohol 13%
Importer Gilbeys
Stockists Tesco · selected Superquinns · Raheny Wine Cellar · Kellys, Clontarf · Mill Wine Cellar, Maynooth · Vineyard, Galway
++

Price about £12 (€15.25)

ALSACE

FRANCE

Domaine Zind Humbrecht Riesling Gueberschwihr Alsace 1997

Everybody's lost count of the number of times Olivier Humbrecht has been named Winemaker of the Year. Intense, flavoursome but light-footed wines like this explain why. Talk about excitement! It has so much body and impact that every mouthful seems to last for minutes, yet it dances gossamer-light across the tongue.

Grape Riesling
Alcohol 13%
Importer Comans
Stockists Vintry, Rathgar · Deveneys, Dundrum · McCabes, Blackrock & Foxrock · On the Grapevine, Dalkey · Jus de Vine, Portmarnock

Price about £15 (€19)

BORDEAUX & THE SOUTHWEST

**Château Jolys Jurançon Sec
1999**

Another wine to look out for if you're in the mood for a full-bodied white with a difference is dry Jurançon, from a little region in the Basque country close to the Pyrenees. In this example, lovely pear-and-pineapple flavours with hints of honey and spice meld in a long, lemony finish.

Grape Gros Manseng
Alcohol 13%
Importer Wines Direct
Stockist Wines Direct

Price about £8.50 (€10.80)

BORDEAUX & THE SOUTHWEST

Château du Seuil Graves Sec
1998

Serious white Bordeaux is bought far more frequently in restaurants than wine shops. Help bring it back to everyday life! This elegant Graves is seamlessly smooth, with a toasty richness that doesn't go overboard and an emphatically firm finish. With fish in a rich sauce, few things could be better.

Grapes Semillon, Sauvignon Blanc
Alcohol 12%
Importer Woodford Bourne
Stockists Mitchells, Kildare St & Glasthule · McCabes, Blackrock & Foxrock · Deveneys, Dundrum · Jus de Vine, Portmarnock +

Price about £15 (€19)

BURGUNDY

**Domaine de la Condemine Mâcon-Péronne Le Clou
Mâcon-Villages 1999**

Mâcon, rich? While plenty on the market represents Burgundy at its most impoverished, this one demonstrates just how fat and luscious this southern Burgundian appellation's wines can be. Made from super-ripe grapes harvested late, it offers intense, honey-streaked flavours, all smoothly knitted together with no oak.

Grape Chardonnay
Alcohol 13%
Importer Wines Direct
Stockist Wines Direct

Price about £9.50 (€12.60)

F R A N C E

BURGUNDY

FRANCE

Domaine Guillemot-Michel Mâcon-Villages Quintaine 1999

Handcrafted by a pair of perfectionists who follow biodynamic principles, this is probably the best Macon I've ever tasted. With gloriously pure, honey-streaked fruit against a classic mineral backdrop and great persistence of flavour, it may change your view of this mixed-bag southern Burgundy appellation for good.

Grape Chardonnay
Alcohol 13%
Importer Burgundy Direct
Stockists Burgundy Direct (by the case) ·Vintry, Rathgar ·
McCabes, Blackrock & Foxrock · Magic Carpet, Cornelscourt ·
On the Grapevine, Dalkey ·Wicklow Wine Co. +

Price £13–£14 (€16.50–€17.80)

1999

Pierrette et Marc
GUILLEMOT- MICHEL
Quintaine

MACON - VILLAGE
APPELLATION CONTRÔLÉE
71260 Clessé - France

ALC 13% BY VOL 750 ML
WINE   PRODUCT OF FRANCE   13% vol 750 ml
VIN

BURGUNDY

Domaine Emilian Gillet Mâcon-Viré Quintaine 1998

From Jean Thévenet, the man who showed Mâcon producers how to get into the super-league by leaving their grapes to ripen until the last second, here's another stunning wine to prove that Burgundy can turn out rich wines without a trace of oak. Peachy, honeyed yet beautifully fresh, it dances on the palate.

Grape Chardonnay
Alcohol 12.8%
Importer Wines Direct
Stockist Wines Direct

Price about £17 (€21.60)

FRANCE

FRANCE

LOIRE

**Château Gaudrelle Vouvray
1999**

Intense flavours of honey, ripe apples and lemon make dry Vouvray one of the most alluring of the richer whites (though sadly it remains one of the most misunderstood). This creamy-textured version, fermented slowly in old oak barriques, is well worth trying. Sensational with gravlax - or alone as an aperitif.

Grape Chenin Blanc
Alcohol 12.5%
Importer James Nicholson
Stockists James Nicholson Direct · Redmonds, Ranelagh · Duffys, Terenure · McCabes, Blackrock & Foxrock · Raheny Wine Cellar · Mill, Maynooth

Price about £10.50 (€13.35)

LOIRE

Marc Brédif Vouvray
1999

And here's one more Vouvray, the mere thought of which sets me salivating. This refined example of Loire Chenin Blanc makes most New World efforts seem like leaden-footed wannabes. With intense citrus flavours and bracing acidity, it unleashes its power in a long, echoing crescendo. Dazzling.

Grape Chenin Blanc
Alcohol 12.5%
Importer Morgans
Stockists McCabes, Blackrock & Foxrock · Higgins, Clonskeagh · On the Grapevine, Dalkey · Martins, Fairview · Greenacres, Wexford +

Price £10-£11 (€12.70-€13.95)

FRANCE

RHÔNE

**Belleruche Côtes-du-Rhône
M. Chapoutier 1999**

The entire Chapoutier operation is biodynamic (meaning organic and a bit more) - right down to high-volume, everyday wines like Belleruche. Some feat. Whether you accept the principles of this rigorous approach or not, there's no doubt that this peachy, easy-going wine has strikingly pure flavours. Belleruche red Côtes-du-Rhône is recommended on page 99.

Grapes Grenache Blanc, Clairette, Bourboulenc
Alcohol 13.5%
Importer Grants of Ireland
Stockists widely available

Price about £7.50 (€9.50)

RHÔNE

FRANCE

Guigal Côtes-du-Rhône
1999/2000

Impeccable house wine, desert-island wine . . . call it what you like, but Guigal's basic white is one of those bottles you keep giving thanks for. It has character and style. It never seems out of place. And, with a hefty portion of Viognier now in the blend, it has lovely, ripe, fruity flavours that make people who rarely enjoy wine sip it and smile. Guigal red Côtes-du-Rhône is recommended on page 137.

Grapes Grenache Blanc, Clairette, Viognier
Alcohol 13%
Importer Barry & Fitzwilliam
Stockists Superquinn and many independent off-licences

Price £9–£9.50 (€11.45–€12)

RHÔNE

**Perrin Réserve Côtes-du-Rhône
1999**

From the organic, dynamic Perrin brothers - owners of Châteauneuf's famous property Beaucastel (see also page 98) - comes this smooth-textured and wonderfully flavoursome but fresh, peach-and-pear-tinged white. Worth trying when you feel in need of a change.

Grapes Grenache Blanc, Bourboulenc, Marsanne, Roussanne, Viognier
Alcohol 13%
Importer Allied Drinks
Stockists Sweeneys, Dorset St & Fairview · Cheers-Gibneys, Malahide · Wine World, Waterford · Egans, Drogheda · Galvins, Cork +

Price £9-£9.50 (€11.45-€12)

SOUTH

Virginie Roussanne
Vin de Pays d'Oc 2000

Although Roussanne is deeply trendy as a stand-alone grape in
California, it still keeps a low profile in Europe, slipping quietly into
white, southern-French blends. Here's an honourable exception
- a fat and lusciously fruity wine with peach, pineapple and honey-
suckle notes. Another great wine to reach for when you're ready
to give Chardonnay a rest.

Grape Roussanne
Alcohol 12.5%
Importer Findlater
Stockists Mitchells, Kildare St & Glasthule · SuperValu,
Drogheda · Wine Centre, Kilkenny · Pettitts in southeast +

Price £6.50-£7 (€8.25-€8.90)

FRANCE

FRANCE

SOUTH

Domaine de Montplaisir Chardonnay-Viognier Cuvée Prestige, Vin de Pays d'Oc 2000

Lob a bit of Viognier into ordinary old Chardonnay and what do you get? A substantial white wine with glorious, subtle hints of peach and apricot, with any luck. With vital freshness in the finish also in its favour, this one is especially tasty with gently spicy food.

Grapes Chardonnay, Viognier
Alcohol 13%
Importer T. P. Reynolds
Stockists SuperValus · Centras · Roches Stores

Price about £8 (€10)

SOUTH

**Domaine de Martinolles Chardonnay
Vin de Pays de l'Aude 2000**

Although I'm definitely suffering from Chardonnay overload (particularly where big, fat monsters are concerned), I find this assertive example undeniably delicious. Stand by for a weighty mouthful of sun-ripened fruit balanced with brilliant acidity. Rich but refreshing, it has a classy, lingering finish. The equally exuberant Martinolles Pinot Noir is recommended on page 102.

Grape Chardonnay
Alcohol 12.5%
Importer Burgundy Direct
Stockists Burgundy Direct (by the case) · Vintry, Rathgar · Michael's Wines, Mount Merrion · Magic Carpet, Cornelscourt · McCabes, Blackrock & Foxrock · Wicklow Wine Co. +

Price £8-£8.50 (€10-€10.80)

GERMANY

Carl Ehrhard Rüdesheimer Berg Rottland Riesling Auslese Trocken, Rheingau 1999

Ah, Germany, why can't you give us more memorable bottles like this? Richly reminiscent of apricots, oranges, honey and candied peel, this divine wine has enough spine-tingling acidity to leave the palate reinvigorated - thirsty even - and its impact lasts for minutes at a time. Still young and taut, it will keep for years. A treat. Just enjoy it on its own.

Grape Riesling
Alcohol 14%
Importer Karwig Wines
Stockists Karwig Wines, Carrigaline · Molloys

Price about £20 (€25.40)

Disnókö Dry Furmint
Tokaji 1997

Here's something deliciously different - a really full-flavoured dry white made from the grape that gives Hungary its dazzling sweet wines. Aromas of pears and peaches with a petrolly edge pave the way for an assertively fruity mouthful with a lingering, spicy finish. An intriguing extrovert with staying power: this vintage still tastes young and fresh.

Grape Furmint
Alcohol 14%
Importer Barry & Fitzwilliam
Stockists selected SuperValus · selected Centras · Cheers-Burnaby, Greystones · Mill, Maynooth +

Price £6.50-£7 (€8.25-€8.90)

HUNGARY

ITALY

Melini Le Grillaie
Vernaccia di San Gimignano 1999

Once you've recovered from the shock of finding an Italian white wine that's big-boned but subtle, you can sit down and enjoy it. Fermented in new oak, it's nutty, as you might expect - but a delicious streak of honey comes as a surprise, with an almond and lemon overlay that's uniquely Italian.

Grape Vernacchia
Alcohol 13%
Importer Gilbeys
Stockists selected Superquinns · Drinkstore, Manor St · Vintry, Rathgar · Martha's Vineyard, Rathfarnham · McCabes, Blackrock & Foxrock · Jus de Vine, Portmarnock +

Price about £9 (€11.50)

Peter Lehmann Barossa Semillon
1999/2000

Back in the days when there was a touch of oak in it, Lehmann's Semillon was a richer white still - but now Australia's best-selling Semillon is lighter, fruitier and very user-friendly, with just a tiny, early hint of the toasty quality this grape gradually develops without going anywhere near a barrel. It'll make you think of homemade lemon curd . . .

Grape Semillon
Alcohol 12.5%
Importer Comans
Stockists Superquinn · selected SuperValus · selected Centras · Roches Stores · Molloys · Bennetts, Howth · Londis, Malahide · Costcutter, Taylor's Lane · Egans, Drogheda +++

Price about £8 (€10)

AUSTRALIA

Château Tahbilk Marsanne
Goulburn Valley 1998

Tahbilk is not merely one of Australia's oldest family-run wineries but the home of the best-known Marsanne in the New World - a rare speciality. Unctuously smooth and exotically flavoured with ripe pineapple, lemon and marzipan, this big, rich wine will age for decades, growing ever more hedonistic. Great, in its youth, with creamy curries.

Grape Marsanne
Alcohol 13%
Importer Comans
Stockists selected Superquinns · Molloys · Sweeneys, Dorset St & Fairview · Kellys, Artane · Cooneys, Harold's Cross · O'Donovans, Cork ++

Price about £9 (€11.50)

Brokenwood Harlequin Unwooded Chardonnay-Verdelho, South Eastern Australia 1999

The minute you lay hold of this, try to organise some chicken satay. Spectacular synergy! The sweet peanut sauce harmonises perfectly with this extravagantly fruity wine, in which honey-streaked mangoes, ripe pineapple and other tropical tastes segue into a refreshing grapefruit finish. It goes really well with mild-to-medium Indian dishes, too. And what an aperitif!

Grapes Chardonnay, Verdelho
Alcohol 13%
Importer Oddbins
Stockist Oddbins

Price about £10 (€12.70)

Mount Pleasant Elizabeth Hunter Valley Semillon, McWilliams 1997

Classic Hunter Valley Semillon is very, very different. Sniffing it, you'll maybe think of preserved lemons or roasted cashews. Those flavours come through powerfully in an unoaked wine which tastes rich yet feels miraculously light and fresh in the mouth - and they linger beautifully. In Semillon terms, this vintage is still a baby. In a few years it will grow smokier, richer, even more alluring.

Grape Semillon
Alcohol 11%
Importer TDL
Stockists Superquinn · Foxs, Grafton St · McCabes, Blackrock & Foxrock · McHughs, Kilbarrack · Mill Wine Cellar, Maynooth · Vineyard, Galway +

Price about £12.50 (€15.90)

Devil's Lair Chardonnay
Margaret River 1999

You won't find many Australian Chardonnays in this book, because they're simply not my thing - but here is a winning exception. From Western Australia (home of Leeuwin Estate, my favourite Aussie Chardonnay, but madly unaffordable), it's stylish in a restrained sort of way, with glorious creamy depth and a long, undulating finish.

Grape Chardonnay
Alcohol 13.5%
Importer Oddbins
Stockist Oddbins

Price about £18 (€22.90)

CHILE

Cono Sur Viognier
Rapel 2000

Luscious apricot, peach and melon flavours, perked up by lively acidity, make this ripe and fruity Chilean a classic Viognier at a great price. Try it on its own, as an aperitif, or with some light, vaguely oriental food - chicken korma, for instance, or just about any Chinese chicken or prawn dish. Cono Sur Pinot Noir is recommended on page 122.

Grape Viognier
Alcohol 13.5%
Importer Superquinn
Stockist Superquinn

Price about £7.50 (€9.50)

NEW ZEALAND

**Villa Maria Reserve Wairau Valley Sauvignon Blanc
Marlborough 1999/2000**

It may seem strange to include a New Zealand Sauvignon in the Richer Whites section, but the flagship version from Villa Maria is a big wine - rich, concentrated and powerful. It carries its weight easily, though, unleashing herbaceous charm by degrees, along with generous grapefruity breadth.

Grape Sauvignon Blanc
Alcohol 14%
Importer Allied Drinks
Stockists Berry Bros, Harry St · McCabes, Blackrock & Foxrock · Pottery Vine, Cabinteely · Egans, Drogheda · Galvins, Cork +

Price £14-£15 (€17.80-€19)

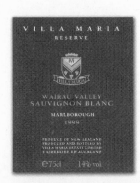

Bonterra Chardonnay
Mendocino County, Fetzer 1999

From the Fetzer organic range, this one-time blockbuster Chardonnay is now being made in a more subtle, middle-of-the-road style, with a switch from American to French oak. Given its firm finish with a dusting of white pepper, this is definitely a wine for food. Bonterra Cabernet Sauvignon features on page 213.

Grape Chardonnay
Alcohol 13.5%
Importer Edward Dillon
Stockists Tesco · selected SuperValus · selected Centras · Roches Stores +++

Price about £12 (€15.25)

Murphy-Goode Barrel-Fermented Chardonnay Sonoma 1998

California's sunshine tends to turn out Chardonnays that seem too in-your-face for European tastes, but this one oozes breeding and simple elegance. We're talking Calvin Klein rather than Oscar de la Renta, in other words. Creamy and slightly nutty with wonderfully persistent flavours, it has enough lively freshness to hold its appeal.

Grape Chardonnay
Alcohol 13.5%
Importer Wines Direct
Stockist Wines Direct

Price about £14 (€17.80)

NORTH AMERICA

NORTH AMERICA

Marimar Torres Estate Chardonnay
Russian River Valley 1998

Fastidiousness characterises everything about the Marimar Torres operation in California, and it shows in the wines - so, although they're expensive, they are genuinely classy. This is a subtly powerful Chardonnay, moving from citrussy charm to lingering buttery richness and firmness.

Grape Chardonnay
Alcohol 13.5%
Importer Woodford Bourne
Stockists Mitchells, Kildare St & Glasthule · Redmonds, Ranelagh · McCabes, Blackrock · Jus de Vine, Portmarnock · Macs, Limerick · Vineyard, Galway +

Price £22-£25 (€28-€32)

Blue White Chenin Blanc, Stellenbosch
Old Vines 1998

The blue bottle somehow suggests a light wine, but don't be fooled. This is one of the most full-on and sensual of all the Chenins coming out of South Africa - a hugely fruity, generous mouthful of ripe lemons and honeyed apples balanced by terrific acidity. Team it with a Thai green curry, Chinese food, barbecued chicken ...

Grape Chenin Blanc
Alcohol 14%
Importer Barry & Fitzwilliam
Stockists selected Superquinns · Raheny Wine Cellar · McCabes, Blackrock & Foxrock · Jus de Vine, Portmarnock · Egans Food Hall, Drogheda · Macs, Limerick +

Price about £8 (€10)

SOUTH AFRICA

L'Avenir Chenin Blanc
Stellenbosch 1999/2000

They're serious, at L'Avenir Estate, about elevating Chenin Blanc from maid-of-all-work to dramatic prima donna. This is an exotic, big-hearted wine whose flavours veer towards tropical richness - passion fruit, pineapple, guavas. The attack is fresh, the texture super and the finish long and citrussy. Try it with a vegetable or chicken curry.

Grape Chenin Blanc
Alcohol 14%
Importer Dunnes Stores
Stockists Dunnes Stores leading outlets

Price about £8 (€10)

Hamilton Russell Vineyards Chardonnay
Walker Bay 1999

A passionate believer in terroir, Anthony Hamilton Russell makes wines with a mineral complexity reminiscent of Burgundy, and every vintage is distinctively different - something you don't always see in the New World. This Chardonnay is an intricate weave of lemon, buttered toast and taut mineral tones, with superb length and polish. Its Pinot Noir partner is lauded on page 220.

Grape Chardonnay
Alcohol 13%
Importer Gilbeys
Stockists Vintry, Rathgar · Martha's Vineyard, Rathfarnham · Higgins, Clonskeagh · McHughs, Kilbarrack · Greenacres, Wexford · De Vine Wines, Letterkenny ++

Price about £17 (€21.60)

SOUTH AFRICA

CHILE

Miguel Torres Santa Digna Cabernet Sauvignon Rosé Curicó 2000

It takes a Spaniard to get Chile working on its pink potential. Fragrantly fruity in a distinctive blackcurrant-and-cassis, Cabernet way, this one's ultra-ripe and relatively full-bodied, but a nice sherbet tang should keep you pouring. Good value, especially as it's often on special offer.

Grape Cabernet Sauvignon
Alcohol 13.5%
Importer Woodford Bourne
Stockists Molloys · selected Cheers Take-Home outlets · selected Next-Door outlets · Limerick Fine Wines · O'Donovans, Cork ++

Price about £8 (€10)

MIGUEL TORRES.
Chile

SANTA DIGNA
2000
Cabernet Sauvignon Rosé
Curicó
Produced and bottled by:
13.5%vol. Soc. Vinícola Miguel Torres, S.A. · Curicó · Product of Chile 75 cl.

BORDEAUX

Château Lacroix Merlot Saignée Rosé
Bordeaux 2000

From significant Englishman-about-Bordeaux Jonathan Malthus, this is a pedigree pink with serious pretensions - a wine to enjoy with a smart summer lunch. Enticing summer pudding aromas lead into a ripe, flavour-packed palate and a long, dry finish. Try it with barbecued lamb (cooked pink, of course).

Grape Merlot
Alcohol 12.5%
Importer Findlater
Stockists McCabes, Blackrock & Foxrock · Redmonds, Ranelagh · Higgins, Clonskeagh · Cheers-Gibneys, Malahide · Kellys, Artane +

Price £8.50-£9 (€10.80-€11.45)

BORDEAUX

FRANCE

Château de Sours Bordeaux Rosé 2000

Over £10 for what seems like a light-hearted, warm-weather wine? Absolutely, if only to discover that really outstanding rosé can stop you in your tracks. This is the Queen of Pinks, *tout court*. Heady aromas of raspberries and blackcurrant leaves, explosive fruit and zippy freshness all linger into the next mouthful. Besides bringing summer dishes to life, it's sensational with Chinese food.

Grape Merlot
Alcohol 13%
Importer Woodford Bourne
Stockists many SuperValus · many Centras · Mitchells, Kildare St & Glasthule · Redmonds, Ranelagh · McCabes, Blackrock · Limerick Fine Wines ++

Price about £11 (€14)

SOUTH

Fortant de France Syrah Rosé
Vin de Pays d'Oc 2000

It's easy to be sniffy about the high-volume Fortant range, churned out in factory-like quantities by Midi big businessman Robert Skalli. But as summer quaffers, the wines offer both value and personality. I especially like the rosé. Tangy, herbal and flavoursome (Syrah makes assertive pinks), it's a modestly priced winner with Mediterranean food.

Grape Syrah
Alcohol 12.5%
Importer Irish Distillers
Stockists SuperValus · Centras · Roches Stores · Molloys ++

Price £6-£6.50 (€7.60-€8.25)

FRANCE

SOUTH

Château de Flaugergues Rosé
Coteaux du Languedoc La Méjanelle 1999/2000

Besides making a very serious, oak-matured red wine (see page 150), Flaugergues puts out this deliciously frivolous rosé. A very pretty shade of pale pink and delicately fruity, it's the sort of thing you can knock back pleasurably on a summer's day, with food or without.

Grapes Grenache, Syrah, Mourvèdre
Alcohol 13.5%
Importer Dunnes Stores
Stockists Dunnes Stores leading outlets

Price £6-£6.50 (€7.60-€8.25)

SOUTH

Bergerie de l'Hortus Rosé de Saignée
Pic Saint Loup 2000

From Jean Orliac, a man who's also given us a brilliantly appetising, summery white (see page 20) and a light, fruity red (see page 101), this constitutes a hat trick. A really classy rosé - gentle and subtly persistent, it leaves the palate fresh and thirsty for more.

Grape Grenache
Alcohol 12.5%
Importer Wines Direct
Stockist Wines Direct

Price £7.50-£8 (€9.50-€10.20)

FRANCE

Produit de France

2000

Rosé de Saignée

BERGERIE de L'HORTUS

....

PIC SAINT LOUP
Coteaux du Languedoc
Appellation Coteaux du Languedoc Contrôlée

Mis en bouteille à France - 34270 par Jean Orliac
750 ml   Domaine de l'Hortus - 34270 Valflaunes   12,5 % alc. / vol.

SPAIN

Gran Feudo Rosé, Navarra
Bodegas Julian Chivite 2000

Look for the tall bottle and the glorious colour - more cran-berry than bubble-gum pink. This top seller from Spain (where good Garnacha-based rosé gets the attention it deserves) has delicious strawberry notes and the perky lift of fresh lemon juice. Perfect for a casual lunch in the garden.

Grape Garnacha
Alcohol 12.5%
Importer TDL
Stockists widely available

Price about £7 (€8.90)

**Enate Rosado Cabernet Sauvignon
Somontano 2000**

SPAIN

Here's proof that France is not the only country to go all per-
nickety about quality pinks. From a progressive winery in the
up-and-coming little region of Somontano, tucked beneath the
Pyrenees, this is Spanish rosé at its most sophisticated - deliciously fresh with a rewardingly long, dry finish.

Grape Cabernet Sauvignon
Alcohol 13%
Importer Fèbvre
Stockists Redmonds, Ranelagh · McCabes, Blackrock &
Foxrock · Cuisine de Vendange, Naas · Terrys, Limerick ·
Lonergans, Clonmel · Hartes, Clonakilty +

Price about £12 (€15.25)

ENATE

ROSADO
CABERNET SAUVIGNON

2000
SOMONTANO
Denominación de Origen

BORDEAUX

FRANCE

Château de la Couronne
Côtes du Marmandais 1999

There's no doubt that some of the lesser-known satellite regions of Bordeaux are worth combing for wines that offer eye-popping value. Although very light in style, this succulent, savoury Côtes du Marmandais has the true Bordeaux character that eludes so many of the region's cheapies.

Grapes Merlot, Cabernet Sauvignon, Cabernet Franc
Alcohol 12%
Importer Musgrave
Stockists SuperValus · Centras · Roches Stores

Price about £6 (€7.60)

BORDEAUX

Berrys' Own Selection Good Ordinary Claret
NV

The bestselling wine by far in Berrys' portfolio is a classic red Bordeaux from the light end of the spectrum, with a distinctly savoury personality despite the blackcurrany Cabernet element. Like almost all the Berrys' Own Selection wines, it is non-vintage - or rather, multi-vintage: blended to achieve consistency year on year.

Grapes Cabernet Sauvignon, Merlot
Alcohol 12%
Importer Berry Bros
Stockist Berry Bros, Harry St

Price about £7 (€8.90)

FRANCE

Established in the XVII Century

BERRY BROS & RUDD LTD
3. ST JAMESS ST LONDON.

GOOD ORDINARY
CLARET

BEAUJOLAIS & BURGUNDY

FRANCE

Saint-Amour Les Bonnets
J-B Patissier 1999

Beaujolais doesn't set my heart aflame, often seeming over-priced for the simple, fruity, young wine that it usually is - so I rarely recommend it. This juicy Saint-Amour offers decent value, however. Forget about the Valentine's Day promotions: knock it back, slightly chilled, any time.

Grape Gamay
Alcohol 13%
Importer Dunnes Stores
Stockists Dunnes Stores leading outlets

Price under £9 (€11.45)

BEAUJOLAIS & BURGUNDY

**Tesco Red Burgundy Bourgogne Pinot Noir
1999**

Fragrant and inviting as a summer compote of red fruits, this soft, uncomplicated Burgundy is dangerously easy to enjoy. Daisy-fresh on the palate with gentle tannins and a juicy finish, it captures the pure charm of young Pinot Noir. Try it chilled in the unlikely event of a heatwave.

Grape Pinot Noir
Alcohol 12.5%
Importer Tesco
Stockist Tesco

Price about £8 (€10)

BEAUJOLAIS & BURGUNDY

**Bourgogne Hautes-Côtes de Beaune
Pierre Ponnelle 1998**

Another unpretentious light Burgundy that offers far more interest and appeal than you might expect, given its modest price tag. Delicately scented with red fruits, herbs and a little pinch of spice, it's succulently juicy with a surprisingly persistent, firm finish.

Grape Pinot Noir
Alcohol 12.5%
Importer Dunnes Stores
Stockists Dunnes Stores leading outlets

Price about £9 (€11.45)

BEAUJOLAIS & BURGUNDY

FRANCE

Bourgogne Pinot Noir
Louis Jadot 1998/1999

In the great minefield of Burgundy, booby-trapped from end to end with indifferent wines at lethal prices, Jadot is a name to cherish for reliability. What I love about this wine is that, even though it's inexpensive (for Burgundy, remember), it displays typical Burgundian charm in a light and lively body. Deliciously subtle.

Grape Pinot Noir
Alcohol 12.5%
Importer Grants of Ireland
Stockists selected SuperValus · O'Briens · Martins, Fairview · Higgins, Clonskeagh · Vineyard, Galway · Lynchs, Glanmire +

Price about £10 (€12.70)

BEAUJOLAIS & BURGUNDY

**Bourgogne Vieilles Vignes, Domaine Vincent Dancer
1999**

From his base at Chassagne-Montrachet, Vincent Dancer turns out a straight, red Burgundy that outstrips many a smarter appellation for concentration and sheer verve. Headily perfumed with raspberries and loganberries, it's vibrantly fruity but reveals real depth mid-palate - and the length is exquisite.

Grape Pinot Noir
Alcohol 12%
Importer Burgundy Direct
Stockists Burgundy Direct (by the case) · Vintry, Rathgar · Michael's Wines, Mount Merrion · McCabes, Blackrock & Foxrock · On the Grapevine, Dalkey · Wicklow Wine Co. +

Price £11-£12 (€14-€15.25)

BEAUJOLAIS & BURGUNDY

**Givry Premier Cru Clos de la Servoisine
Domaine Joblot 1999/2000**

Radical grower Jean-Marc Joblot coaxes wonderfully ripe, seductive reds from the Côte Chalonnaise, an area somewhat eclipsed by grander appellations. Here is a beguiling example - a heady young wine layered with flavour and intrigue. Fruity and supple, Givry reds sit at the lighter end of the Burgundy spectrum, but this is no wimp.

Grape Pinot Noir
Alcohol 13%
Importer Burgundy Direct
Stockists Burgundy Direct (by the case) · Vintry, Rathgar · McCabes, Blackrock & Foxrock · Magic Carpet, Cornelscourt · On the Grapevine, Dalkey · Wicklow Wine Co. +

Price £15-£17 (€19-€21.60)

F R A N C E

FRANCE

LOIRE

Marc Brédif Chinon
1999

This light and refreshing Loire red would be perfect for a spring or summer lunch. Beguiling aromas of raspberries and black-berries lead into a palate laden with soft berry fruits, but striking acidity and firmness in the long, bone-dry finish make this a wine for food.

Grape Cabernet Franc
Alcohol 12.5%
Importer Morgans
Stockists Molloys · Higgins, Clonskeagh · Cheers-Baily, Howth · Jus de Vine, Portmarnock · On the Grapevine, Dalkey +

Price £10-£11 (€12.70-€13.95)

LOIRE

Saumur-Champigny Vieilles Vignes
Domaine Filliatreau 1998

Loire reds are reputedly difficult to sell to Irish palates, but this engaging example has built up a following of entranced fans - maybe because its grapes from old vines give it richer, more concentrated flavours than is usual. A wine to perk up jaded palates, it fuses the fresh tang of Cabernet Franc with blackberries and spice - without recourse to oak. Food is vital with this one, too.

Grape Cabernet Franc
Alcohol 12.5%
Importer J & T Davy
Stockists Searsons, Monkstown · On the Grapevine, Dalkey · Wine Centre, Kilkenny · Ryan Vine, Navan +

Price about £15 (€19)

FRANCE

RHÔNE

La Vieille Ferme
Côtes du Ventoux 1999

The Perrin brothers of top-ranking Châteauneuf property Beaucastel (see also page 60) encourage the growers who supply the grapes for their everyday wines to follow organic methods. Could that be why this fruity, lightly spiced red tastes so vibrant? It's excellent value and very user-friendly.

Grapes Grenache, Syrah, Cinsault, Mourvèdre
Alcohol 12.5%
Importer Allied Drinks
Stockists widely available

Price about £7.50 (€9.50)

RHÔNE

Belleruche Côtes-du-Rhône
M. Chapoutier 1999

It's unusual to find a white-and-red duo in which both wines hold equal appeal, but the berry-ripe, herb-tinged Belleruche red is every bit as engaging as the peachy white (see page 58). Not merely organic but biodynamic, its pure fruit flavours sing on the palate. A fruity, pretty Côtes-du-Rhône.

Grapes Grenache, Syrah
Alcohol 13.5%
Importer Grants of Ireland
Stockists Superquinn · many SuperValus · many Centras · some Tesco outlets · Pettitts in the southeast +++

Price £8-£8.50 (€10-€10.80)

SOUTH

Domaine de Montplaisir Merlot
Vin de Pays d'Oc 1999

Here's an Old World Merlot with plenty of sun-ripened, southern-French fruit, but maybe a little more intrigue than we've come to expect of Chilean Merlots at a comparable price. Smooth, lively and relatively light, it has hints of plum compote, vegetal undertones and a dusting of spice.

Grape Merlot
Alcohol 12.5%
Importer Musgraves
Stockists SuperValus · Centras · Roches Stores

Price about £6 (€7.60)

SOUTH

Bergerie de l'Hortus Classique
Pic Saint Loup 1999

Deep in the Languedoc, impassioned Jean Orliac has cracked the
secret of making wines that have immediate appeal and lingering
interest. A rare enough feat! This tempting, flexible red makes a
fine trio with the white recommended on page 20 and the rosé
on page 85. Succulent and inviting, it evokes the medley of red
fruits in a summer pudding, but a savoury core adds an extra
dimension.

Grapes Syrah, Mourvèdre, Grenache
Alcohol 12.5%
Importer Wines Direct
Stockist Wines Direct

Price about £8.50 (€10.80)

Product de France

2000

CLASSIQUE

BERGERIE de L'HORTUS

....

Vin de Pays de
Val de Montferrand

Mis en bouteille à France - 1979 par Jean Orliac
750 ml   Domaine de l'Hortus - 1979 Valflaunes   12.5 % alc. / vol

SOUTH

FRANCE

**Domaine de Martinolles Pinot Noir
Vin de Pays de l'Aude 1999**

From a super Languedoc estate, whose Chardonnay is recommended on page 63, this light, deliciously fruity red is perfect for summer drinking. Commendably less jammy than most Pinots from the south of France, it's more like a prettily perfumed, raspberryish young Burgundy. Except, of course, for the price.

Grape Pinot Noir
Alcohol 13.5%
Importer Burgundy Direct
Stockists Burgundy Direct (by the case) ·Vintry, Rathgar ·
Michael's Wines, Mount Merrion · McCabes, Blackrock &
Foxrock · Magic Carpet, Cornelscourt ·Wicklow Wine Co. +

Price £8.50-£9 (€10.80-€11.45)

**Tsantali Nemea
1998**

One of the greatest wine bargains in Ireland languishes on the shelves under-appreciated - because too many people remember too many awful Greek holiday wines. This is an enticing light red with soft, jammy, vanilla-infused fruit and the sort of juicy nature that leads to empty bottles. It's easy to knock back on its own.

Grape Agiorgitiko
Alcohol 12%
Importer Hellenic Marketing
Stockist Dunnes Stores

Price about £5 (€6.35)

GREECE

Agiorgitiko Boutari
Nemea 1999

Another Shirley Valentine bottle to tempt you into having a Greek fling! While many red wines from warm countries are more syrupy than the sickliest romance, this one is light, elegant and low in alcohol. With a nice, refreshing tang in the finish, it's a red custom-made for summer.

Grape Agiorgitiko
Alcohol 12%
Importer Irish Distillers
Stockists selected Superquinns · selected Cheers Take-Home outlets · Redmonds, Ranelagh · Mulqueens, Nenagh · O'Haras, Foxford +

Price £8-£8.50 (€10-€10.80)

PRODUCT OF GREECE

Agiorgitiko Boutari
1999
Dry red wine
APPELLATION OF ORIGIN NEMEA OF HIGH QUALITY

750 ml BOUTARI Alc. 12%/Vol.
ESTABLISHED 1879
PRODUCED & BOTTLED BY: A.K.M.09-0014/99 J. BOUTARI & SON · THESSALONIKI, GREECE

D'Istinto Sangiovese-Merlot
Sicilia 1999

Made in Sicily by Australian giant BRL Hardy, the red D'Istinto has
the same, easy charm as the white (see page 23) while holding
on firmly to its Italian personality. Merlot lends a soft edge to the
tangy palate of cherries and herbs, but there's a nice little bitter-
sweet Sangiovese twist in the tail. A lip-smacking bargain.

Grapes Sangiovese, Merlot
Alcohol 12.5%
Importer Allied Drinks
Stockists SuperValus · Centras · Pettitts in southeast +++

Price about £6 (€7.60)

ITALY

Santa Cristina Toscana
Antinori 1999

Not one of your thin, bitter Italian cheapies: this is a nice, rounded mouthful. Unless I'm dreaming, Santa Cristina isn't quite as light a wine as it used to be; it seems a touch smoother, richer, almost chocolate-edged. It's still relatively light, all the same. Perfect with white meats, pizza, pasta and the like.

Grapes Sangiovese, Merlot
Alcohol 12.5%
Importer Grants of Ireland
Stockists widely available

Price £7-£7.50 (€8.90-€9.50)

Masi Valpolicella Classico Superiore
1999

Good Valpolicella is still confused, alas, with the worst student-party poison. Although straightforward and inexpensive, this is the real McCoy - and very superior it is to a lot of Valpol on the shelves. Super-smooth and fruity, it has a nice little nip of classic Italian bitter-cherry character in the finish without being tart.

Grapes Corvina, Rondinella, Molinara
Alcohol 12%
Importer Grants of Ireland
Stockists widely available

Price about £7.50 (€9.50)

ITALY

Villa Rizzardi Poiega Valpolicella Classico Superiore 1999

From an organic producer, this Valpol is so light in style that you may be inclined to dismiss it. Big mistake. All sorts of subtle flavours emerge, by degrees, from that svelte body - cherries, herbs, mineral hints, earthy tones, zingy freshness. The longer you sip it, the more you'll enjoy it.

Grapes Corvina, Rondinella, Molinara, Negrara
Alcohol 12.5%
Importer Irish Distillers
Stockists McCabes, Blackrock · Vintry, Rathgar · Redmonds, Ranelagh · Sweeneys, Dorset St · Pettitts in southeast · O'Donovans, Cork +

Price £9-£9.50 (€11.45-€12)

**Cabernet Roncaccio, Friuli
Collavini 1998**

Something distinctively different from northeastern Italy. In the hands of Collavini, producers of an ever-tempting Pinot Grigio (see page 26), Cabernets Sauvignon and Franc make a light, elegant, juicy red with minty aromas and a silky texture. Anybody who finds the bitter-cherry character of many Italian reds hard to take should plunge into this with relief.

Grapes Cabernet Sauvignon, Cabernet Franc
Alcohol 13%
Importer Woodford Bourne
Stockists selected Superquinns · Claudio's Wines, Drury St · Redmonds, Ranelagh · Fine Wines, Limerick · Greenacres, Wexford · O'Donovans, Cork +

Price about £10 (€12.70)

PORTUGAL

**Periquita, Vinho Regional Terras do Sado
J M da Fonseca 1997**

With its wafts of strawberry jam and caramel, this appealing Portuguese red may remind you of a good, everyday Rioja - except for its knockdown price. Soft, fruity, engaging and different, it's easy to look out for if you remember that Periquita, the name of both the grape and the wine, means parakeet or little parrot.

Grape Periquita
Alcohol 12%
Importer Gilbeys
Stockists selected Superquinns · selected SuperValus · selected Centras · Pettitts in southeast +++

Price £7.50-£8 (€9.50-€10)

SPAIN

Gran Feudo Crianza, Navarra
Bodegas Julian Chivite 1997

Unlike some of our fruity friends from the New World, this is a wine you won't easily tire of - and it's also further proof of how important Spain now is as a source of well-priced, interesting wines. Suggestions of leather and herbs add intrigue to ripe, brambly fruit flavours. A brilliant mid-week buy.

Grapes Tempranillo, Garnacha, Cabernet Sauvignon
Alcohol 12.5%
Importer TDL
Stockists widely available

Price about £7.50 (€9.50)

SPAIN

Ochoa Tempranillo Crianza
Navarra 1997

The first ever *Irish Times* 'Bottle of the Week', way back when, and it remains a top nomination for everyday drinking in the current vintage. In this juicily inviting wine, those few years of maturity make for well-integrated flavours - dark berries, a puff of smoke, a touch of leather - and nice, supple tannins.

Grape Tempranillo
Alcohol 12.5%
Importer Kelly & Co
Stockists widely available

Price about £8 (€10)

Can Vendrell Cabernet Sauvignon-Tempranillo, Penedès, Albet i Noya 1999/2000

Josep Albet is one of the young generation of winemakers who are shaking up the Spanish wine scene. He's committed to organic methods, and every one of his wines has remarkably pure, zingy flavours. This, the entry-level red, is light, lively and extremely likeable.

Grapes Tempranillo, Garnacha, Cabernet Sauvignon, Cariñena
Alcohol 12.5%
Importer Mary Pawle
Stockists Superquinn · Redmonds, Ranelagh · Sweeneys, Dorset St · Good Food Store, Pembroke Lane · Fields, Skibbereen · Organico, Bantry +

Price about £8 (€10)

CAN VENDRELL
de la Codina

CABERNET SAUVIGNON
& TEMPRANILLO

2000

PENEDÈS
denominació d'origen

PRODUCT OF SPAIN
ORGANICALLY GROWN I ÖKOLOGISCHER ANBAU

Torres Sangre de Toro
Catalunya 1999

There's a tendency to bypass this and reach for the swankier
Torres Gran Sangre de Toro. In fact, while the two wines are
very different in style and structure, each is delicious in its way.
This is the soft, gluggable one - a juicy mouthful of raspberries,
damsons and gentle spice. Not exactly a lightweight, but light in
comparison to its big brother.

Grapes Garnacha, Cariñena
Alcohol 13.5%
Importer Woodford Bourne
Stockists widely available

Price under £8 (under €10)

Riscal Tempranillo, Castilla y Leon
Marques de Riscal 1999

Here's a tempting red wine from a bodega well known for its Riojas (and its fresh whites from Rueda, see page 30). Subtle rather than full-blooded, this relatively recent creation marries ripe berry and vanilla flavours with juicy acidity and a firm, savoury finish. Smart - as is the tall bottle in which it comes.

Grape Tempranillo
Alcohol 13%
Importer Findlater
Stockists Higgins, Clonskeagh · McHughs, Kilbarrack · Cheers-Gibneys, Malahide · Pottery Vine, Cabinteely · Cheers-Wicklow Arms, Delgany · Mill Wine Cellar, Maynooth +

Price £8.50-£9 (€10.80-€11.45)

ARGENTINA

Santa Isabel Malbec
Mendoza, Nieto Senetiner 1999

Lighter and more reticent in style than some Argentine Malbecs, this is nevertheless a great buy. Soft and round with ripe, blackberryish fruit, it's easy to get into, yet spicy and savoury notes emerge to keep it at a very safe distance from the bland and boring category. Great for parties.

Grape Malbec
Alcohol 12.5%
Importer Dunnes Stores
Stockists Dunnes Stores

Price under £6 (under €7.60)

Medrano Bonarda
Mendoza 1999

The Italian grape Bonarda is responsible for oceans of utterly forgettable Argentine wine - but here it emerges as a likeable performer. Packed with soft, raspberry flavours and a hint of chocolate, this is the sort of unashamedly fruity, juicy red you could guzzle with simple pleasure just about any time.

Grape Bonarda
Alcohol 12.5%
Importer James Adams
Stockists many independent off-licences

Price about £7 (€8.90)

ARGENTINA

AUSTRALIA

Tyrrell's Old Winery Pinot Noir
Hunter Valley-McLaren Vale-Barossa 1999

I still prefer this simple Pinot Noir from Tyrrells to their fancier (and much oakier) Eclipse. It's all about balance. This one is straightforward and very drinkable - a light and gentle New World Pinot to enjoy with food or without. Especially delicious with spicy dishes, its sweet vanilla-tinged cherry fruit makes it fusion-friendly.

Grape Pinot Noir
Alcohol 13%
Importer Maxxium
Stockists selected SuperValus · selected Centras · Roches Stores · Redmonds, Ranelagh · Cheers-Gibneys, Malahide · Shannon Knights, Shannon · Fine Wines, Limerick ++

Price about £8.50 (€10.80)

Mount Pleasant Philip Hunter Valley Shiraz
McWilliams 1994

While you're on the lookout for Mount Pleasant Elizabeth Semillon (see page 70), keep an eye open for its suave red cousin. This is Shiraz from the discreet end of the spectrum. Layered with sweet fruit, herbs, leather and a light dusting of pepper, it's also rewardingly mature - and look at that civilised alcohol level!

Grape Shiraz
Alcohol 11.5%
Importer TDL
Stockists Foxs, Grafton St · McHughs, Kilbarrack · McCabes, Blackrock & Foxrock · Mill Wine Cellar, Maynooth · Wine Cellar, Portlaoise · Vineyard, Galway +

Price about £12.50 (€15.90)

AUSTRALIA

Ninth Island Pinot Noir
Tasmania, Piper's Brook 2000

Ninth Island is the second label of Tasmania's well-known winery Piper's Brook. (See next page for the splendid Estate Pinot Noir under that name.) Visionary Andrew Pirie knows how to coax both character and charm out of the fickle red grape of Burgundy. This is an easy charmer, with oodles of soft fruit and an almost spritzy tang. It's delicious lightly chilled.

Grape Pinot Noir
Alcohol 13.5%
Importer Irish Distillers
Stockists Kellys, Artane · Londis, Malahide · McCabes, Blackrock & Foxrock · Ashford Food & Wines, Co. Wicklow · Fine Wines, Limerick · O'Donovans, Cork +

Price about £13 (€16.50)

**Piper's Brook Vineyard Estate Pinot Noir
Tasmania 2000**

Maybe it's Tasmania's coolish climate, maybe it's Andrew Pirie's Pinot obsession, maybe it's just Bacchus lending a hand ... but this is one of the most subtle and rewarding of all the New World Pinots seen so far. Fragrant and complex, with gamey and herbal notes, sweet cherry fruit and subtle spice beautifully integrated, it remains light and elegant right down to the last drop.

Grape Pinot Noir
Alcohol 13.5%
Importer Irish Distillers
Stockists Vaughan Johnsons, Temple Bar · McHughs, Kilbarrack · Deveneys, Dundrum · Cheers-Wicklow Arms, Delgany · Mill Wine Cellar, Maynooth · O'Donovans, Cork +

Price £15-£16 (€19-€20.35)

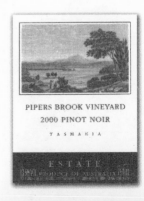

PIPERS BROOK VINEYARD
2000 PINOT NOIR
TASMANIA

ESTATE

CHILE

**Cono Sur Pinot Noir
Rapel 2000**

When you see how many only-just-OK New World Pinots there are at £15-£16, it's incredibly cheering to stumble upon this perky and personable version at about half that price. From an adventurous modern winery (their Viognier is recommended on page 72), it has fragrant aromas of raspberries, cherries and herbs, leading into an appealingly juicy palate.

Grape Pinot Noir
Alcohol 13.5%
Importer Oddbins
Stockist Oddbins

Price about £8 (€10)

CHILE

Canepa Winemaker's Selection Zinfandel Curicó 1999

Most of the Zinfandel we see is (a) Californian and (b) powerful stuff, making this light-hearted Chilean really stand out. From an innovative winery whose latest experiments stretch to Riesling, Sangiovese, Viognier, even Tempranillo, it's deliciously raspberryish and vibrant with overtones of herbs and subtle spice.

Grape Zinfandel
Alcohol 13.5%
Importer MacCormaic
Stockists selected Superquinns · Roches Stores · Cooneys, Harold's Cross · Wine Bottle, Dunshaughlin · Bradleys, Cork · O'Donovans, Cork ++

Price about £8.50 (€10.80)

NEW ZEALAND

Hunter's Pinot Noir
Marlborough 1999

Hunter's Sauvignon Blanc (see page 44) is such a star performer that it seemed unlikely the partnering Pinot Noir, newer to the Irish market, could equal it. It does! A super-lively, seductive Pinot - one of New Zealand's very best - with oak so delicately handled that it lets the exuberant fruit show through.

Grape Pinot Noir
Alcohol 13.5%
Importer Gilbeys
Stockists Drinkstore, Manor St · Martins, Fairview · Jus de Vine, Portmarnock · McCabes, Blackrock · Martha's Vineyard, Rathfarnham · Vineyard, Galway ++

Price about £14 (€17.80)

**Wente Reliz Creek Reserve Pinot Noir
Monterey 1998**

The sweet, almost jammy fruit in this Californian is offset by
good acidity, and interesting notes of herbs and spice emerge in
a gently reverberating finish. The result? A supple Pinot Noir with
easy charm and grace. With all that ripeness and soft tannin, it's
another great candidate for fusion food. Try it lightly chilled.

Grape Pinot Noir
Alcohol 13.5%
Importer Cassidy
Stockists Dunnes Stores leading outlets

Price about £12 (€15.25)

NORTH AMERICA

SOUTH AFRICA

Vaughan Johnson's Good Everyday Cape Red
South Africa, NV

Cape Town's best-known retailer, Vaughan Johnson, built up a successful business by sourcing easy-drinking blends at cracking prices (and then giving them easy names - Sunday Best and Seriously Good Plonk are also in the line-up). Chock full of juicy fruit lightly dusted with pepper and spice, this one races out of his Dublin door to Temple Bar receptions.

Grapes Shiraz, Pinotage, Cabernet, Cinsaut
Alcohol 13%
Importer Papillon
Stockists Vaughan Johnsons, Temple Bar · Wicklow Wine Co. ·
Sky and Ground, Wexford ++

Price about £6 (€7.60)

Vaughan Johnson's
Good Everyday Cape Red
This hearty red is the epitome of a superb house wine. It is rich and bursting with vibrant fruit flavours. Made in the style of the friendly country wines of France it has a smooth texture and an earthy character. Enjoy it now or over the next year or two.
Vaughan
A216   13/Vol
PRODUCE OF SOUTH AFRICA

BORDEAUX & THE SOUTHWEST

Château de la Colline Bergerac
1999

Well-travelled winemaker Charles Martin gives his Bergeracs New World opulence - and his neighbours a major new talking point. Strikingly rich and round with bags of ripe blackcurrant and vanilla, this is for anybody in flight from the weedy, watery reds that sometimes reach us from the greater Bordeaux area at around the same price.

Grapes Cabernet Sauvignon, Merlot, Cabernet Franc
Alcohol 12.5%
Importer Findlater
Stockists Redmonds, Ranelagh · Sweeneys, Dorset St · Cheers-Comet, Santry · Londis, Malahide · Bourkes, Cabinteely · Blessings, Cavan +

Price about £9 (€11.45)

GRAND VIN DU TERROIR

1999 1999

Château de La Colline

BERGERAC
APPELLATION BERGERAC CONTRÔLÉE
MIS EN BOUTEILLE AU CHATEAU

12.5% vol.   Charles R.L. Martin Producteur à Thénac Dordogne   75 cl
Produce of France

FRANCE

BORDEAUX & THE SOUTHWEST

Michel Lynch Bordeaux
1998

Leave Château Lynch-Bages, Ireland's favourite classed growth claret, to the stockbrokers. From the same dynasty, this is a pretty decent everyday substitute for the rest of us. Juicy plums and blackcurrant flavours come first, then just a touch of the chewiness that hints at underlying structure. Quite stylish at the price.

Grapes Cabernet Sauvignon, Merlot
Alcohol 12%
Importer Barry & Fitzwilliam
Stockists widely available

Price about £9 (€11.45)

BORDEAUX & THE SOUTHWEST

**Château Méaume Bordeaux Supérieur
1998**

When Alan and Sue Johnson-Hill took over this modest property 20 years ago, a young man by the name of Michel Rolland was the wine consultant. Even though he's now ridiculously famous, Rolland has stuck with them, helping to create one of the most impressive red Bordeaux under £10. Already delicious, the rich and generous 1998 should keep for quite a few years.

Grapes Merlot, Cabernet Franc, Cabernet Sauvignon
Alcohol 13%
Importer Findlater
Stockists Molloys · Mortons, Ranelagh · Bennetts, Howth · Wine Centre, Kilkenny · Bradleys, Cork · Fahys, Ballina ++

Price £9-£10 (€11.45-€12.70)

BORDEAUX & THE SOUTHWEST

FRANCE

Château Patache d'Aux
Médoc Cru Bourgeois 1997

I've loved this approachable, classic Bordeaux devotedly for years and years. Carefully made by the Lapalu family near the northern tip of the Médoc, it has soft, plummy fruit with a mineral streak and a dash of pepper, good acidity and lovely, supple tannins. Always finely tuned, always tempting. Look out for it in restaurants especially.

Grapes Cabernet Sauvignon, Merlot
Alcohol 12.5%
Importer Grants of Ireland
Stockists Sweeneys, Dorset St & Fairview · SuperValu, Drogheda · Vineyard, Galway +

Price £16-£17 (€20.35-€21.60)

BORDEAUX & THE SOUTHWEST

Château de la Cour Saint-Emilion
1998

From a young winemaker who understands how to appeal to today's drinkers without sacrificing Bordeaux character, this modern, round St Emilion has become a Mitchells bestseller. It's especially tasty with lamb - for there's a touch of mint in there, along with beautifully ripe, liquorice-tinged fruit.

Grapes Merlot, Cabernet Franc
Alcohol 12.5%
Importer Mitchell & Son
Stockist Mitchells, Kildare St & Glasthule

Price about £13 (€16.50)

BORDEAUX & THE SOUTHWEST

FRANCE

Frank Phélan Saint-Estèphe
1998

If you feel like trading up a bit, the second wine of Château Phélan-Segur is a good bet. All the improvements made at this property by the Gardinier brothers are now beginning to show in wines with breeding and refinement. This vintage is strikingly full-bodied, with plummy, velvety fruit, supple tannins and serious allure.

Grapes Cabernet Sauvignon, Merlot, Cabernet Franc
Alcohol 12.5%
Importer Barry & Fitzwilliam
Stockists Redmonds, Ranelagh · Kellys, Artane · Lord Mayor's, Swords · Wine Vault, Portlaoise · Val Manning, Bantry +

Price about £20 (€25.40)

MIS EN BOUTEILLE A LA PROPRIÉTÉ

Frank Phélan
Saint-Estèphe
APPELLATION SAINT-ESTÈPHE CONTRÔLÉE
1998
X. GARDINIER & FILS
CHÂTEAU PHÉLAN SEGUR S.A
PROPRIÉTAIRE A SAINT-ESTÈPHE-GIRONDE-FRANCE
12.5% vol.   Bordeaux - Produit de France   750 ml

BURGUNDY

Savigny-les-Beaune Premier Cru Les Lavières
Charles Viénot 1996

Red Burgundy under £15 (and sometimes well over that price) is often either thin and tart or just pleasantly fruity in a Beaujolais sort of way. This one's a winner, however, both in terms of price and character. Supple and harmonious with ethereal aromas of ripe strawberries, it also hints at those gamey undertones that make Burgundy intriguing. Mellow and long, it's already quite mature, so drink it soon.

Grape Pinot Noir
Alcohol 13%
Importer Superquinn
Stockist Superquinn

Price about £12 (€15.25)

FRANCE

BURGUNDY

**Mercurey Premier Cru Clos des Myglands
Faiveley 1998**

With its heady perfume of raspberries, cherries and herbs -
elements that all explode on the palate with intriguing mineral
undertones - this Burgundy is a hedonist's delight. The firm
tannic structure suggests it will continue to deliver pleasure for
years. A star buy - mainly in restaurants.

Grape Pinot Noir
Alcohol 12.5%
Importer Maxxium
Stockist Berry Bros, Harry St +

Price £19-£20 (€24-€25.40)

BURGUNDY

Aloxe-Corton
Domaine Latour 1996

The house of Latour is so well known for its widely distributed white wines that the sumptuous reds are sometimes overlooked. This is a good example - round and intense with nicely integrated, toasty oak providing a firm, meaty finish. It will keep for another few years but is also divinely drinkable right now.

Grape Pinot Noir
Alcohol 13.5%
Importer Gilbeys
Stockists selected Tescos · Mitchells, Kildare St & Glasthule · Redmonds, Ranelagh · Lord Mayor's, Swords · O'Donovans Cork +

Price about £22 (€27.95)

ALOXE-CORTON
DOMAINE LATOUR
APPELLATION ALOXE-CORTON CONTRÔLÉE

ANNÉE 1996

MIS EN BOUTEILLE PAR LOUIS LATOUR NÉGOCIANT-ÉLEVEUR
LOUIS LATOUR, A BEAUNE (CÔTE-D'OR) - FRANCE
PRODUIT DE FRANCE

BURGUNDY

FRANCE

Volnay
Domaine Michel Lafarge 1998

Enticing wafts of cherries, raspberries, chocolate and damp earth are the prelude. Then the penetrating flavours of this beautifully fleshy Volnay from a master producer break like a wave, leading into a long, powerful finish. Poise, elegance, persistence ... the magic of Burgundy!

Grape Pinot Noir
Alcohol 13%
Importer Burgundy Direct
Stockist Burgundy Direct (by the case) · Vintry, Rathgar · Michael's Wines, Mount Merrion · McCabes, Blackrock & Foxrock · Magic Carpet, Cornelscourt · Wicklow Wine Co. +

Price £22.50–£24 (€28.50–€30.50)

RHÔNE

Guigal Côtes-du-Rhône
1998/1999

Again, this is the red half of an impressive pair. (The white is recommended on page 59.) Although leading Rhône producer Marcel Guigal produces prodigious quantities of his Côtes-du-Rhône, there's no skimping on quality in this juicy, herb-scented, spicey red. One of the great reliables.

Grapes Grenache, Mourvèdre, Syrah
Alcohol 13%
Importer Barry & Fitzwilliam
Stockists Superquinn and many independent off-licences

Price £9-£9.50 (€11.45-€12)

FRANCE

RHÔNE

Rasteau Les Peyrières
Côtes-du-Rhône Villages 1999

If you like 'em big and bold, give this swaggering extrovert a whirl. What it lacks in sophistication (we're dealing here with the rustic end of Rasteau) it makes up for in lush, jammy fruit, warm spice and sheer gutsy attack. And you certainly can't complain about the price.

Grapes Grenache, Syrah, Mourvèdre
Alcohol 14%
Importer Dunnes Stores
Stockists Dunnes Stores leading outlets

Price about £6 (€7.60)

RHÔNE

FRANCE

Louis Bernard
Côtes-du-Rhône Villages 1998

Before the cork was drawn, I was slightly suspicious of this wine in its heavy, old-style bottle. *Le marketing!* My mistake, because this is a terrific buy - a full-bodied, intense, characterful red. Luscious notes of cassis, toasty vanilla and spice firm up in a long, chewy finish.

Grapes Grenache, Syrah, Mourvèdre, Cinsault
Alcohol 13%
Importer O'Briens
Stockist O'Briens

Price about £8 (€10)

FRANCE

RHÔNE

Domaine La Soumade Rasteau
Côtes-du-Rhône Villages 1998/1999

Now for the swankier end of Rasteau. With this remarkably
dense, intense wine, Rhône superstar André Romero demonstrates the potential of this overshadowed little appellation.
Bags of rich, spicy fruit, the mineral echoes of terroir and ripe
tannins make an imposing ensemble.

Grapes Grenache, Syrah, Mourvèdre, Cinsault, Carignan
Alcohol 13.5%
Importer Berry Bros · James Nicholson
Stockists Berry Bros, Harry St · James Nicholson Direct ·
Cheers-Gibneys, Malahide · Mill Wine Cellar, Maynooth · Wicklow
Wine Co. +

Price about £11 (€13.95)

Domaine la Soumade

Rasteau

Côtes du Rhône Villages
APPELLATION CÔTES DU RHÔNE VILLAGES CONTRÔLÉE

13,5%Vol.   *Mis en bouteille au domaine*   750ML
Eng. Romero André propriétaire récoltant à 84110 Rasteau

1999   PRODUCT OF FRANCE   1999

RHÔNE

Crozes-Hermitage Domaine de Thalabert
Jaboulet Aîné 1997

This star performer from the northern Rhône is the sort of wine that would turn almost any winter meal into a treat. Its rich, layered flavours (sweet cherry toffee, undertones of earth) linger on and on . . . at least until the bottle's empty. Super acidity partly accounts for its palate-refreshing appeal.

Grape Syrah
Alcohol 13%
Importer Gilbeys
Stockists Sweeneys, Dorset St · Deveneys, Dundrum · Higgins, Clonskeagh · Jus de Vine, Portmarnock · O'Connors, Salthill ++

Price £17-£18 (€21.60-€22.90)

RHÔNE

Domaine du Vieux Télégraphe
Châteauneuf-du-Pape 1998/1999

The old telegraph keeps sending out better and better signals. This wine may not be a snip, exactly, but it is the sort of treat you will remember. A heady perfume, masses of ripe, rich fruit, a dusting of exotic spices ... If you can bear to keep it a few years (the 1999 is still young and tight), it will mature into a glorious confection of dates, figs and maraschino cherries.

Grapes Syrah, Grenache, Cinsault, Mourvèdre
Alcohol 14%
Importer Findlater
Stockists Berry Bros, Harry St · Cheers-Gibneys, Malahide · Jus de Vine, Portmarnock · Ashford Food & Wines, Co. Wicklow · Old Stand, Mullingar ++

Price £25–£26 (€32–€33)

SOUTH

Château Maris Minervois
Comte Cathare 1998

A hot contender for the title of supreme southern-French bargain red. Bertie Eden, the Englishman who makes this wine, believes passionately in biodynamic viticulture. "Live soil makes live wine!" Certainly this rich, fleshy, flavour-packed example is full of character and verve. As for value, few bottles can equal it. The Eden budget Chardonnay is recommended on page 19.

Grapes Syrah, Grenache, Carignan
Alcohol 13%
Importer Oddbins
Stockist Oddbins

Price about £7 (€8.90)

FRANCE

Domaine de Sainte Marthe Syrah
Vin de Pays de Cassan 2000

Wafts of black fruits, caramel, wood smoke and damp earth announce a swashbuckling wine with heaps of interest. This smooth, fleshy red delivers on the palate, too, with a nice juicy middle and a mocha-edged, lingering finish. Very good drinking at the price, and not a bit too young.

Grape Syrah
Alcohol 12.5%
Importer J. S. Woods
Stockists Listons, Camden St · Vintry, Rathgar · Ryan Vine, Navan · Cheers-Wicklow Arms, Delgany · Pettitts in southeast · Wine Bottle, Dunshaughlin ++

Price about £7.50 (€9.50)

SOUTH

**Jean-Louis Denois Mourvèdre-Grenache
Vin de Pays d'Oc 1999**

Suspend your nose over a glass of this and you'll know from all the earthy oomph that it's a wine with a strapping personality. It tastes even better than it smells. Luscious, dark fruits mingle with gutsy pepper and punch in a lip-smacking finish - and the suede-like, mouth-coating texture is seductive.

Grapes Mourvèdre, Grenache
Alcohol 12.5%
Importer River Wines
Stockist River Wines

Price about £8 (€10)

FRANCE

SOUTH

FRANCE

**Moulin de Gassac Vieilles Vignes Elise
Vin de Pays de l'Hérault 1998**

Masterminded by the irrepressible Aimé Guibert of well-known Mas de Daumas Gassac, this wine and the next have all the individuality and southern-French chutzpah you might expect from the tireless lion of the Languedoc. Elise is smooth and lively, with delicious hints of maraschino cherries, herbs and chocolate in a velvet wrap.

Grapes Merlot, Syrah
Alcohol 12.5%
Importer O'Briens
Stockist O'Briens

Price about £8 (€10)

SOUTH

Moulin de Gassac Vieilles Vignes Albaran
Vin de Pays de l'Hérault 1998

Compared to Elise, the previous wine, Albaran is bigger in structure - a brawny, muscular monsieur, if we're allowed to be sexist, rather than an elegant madame. But it, too, has a wonderfully sweet, rich side to its nature. You'll detect hints of dates, figs and liquorice in this dark lothario. Sensational with a winter roast or stew.

Grapes Cabernet Sauvignon, Mourvèdre, Syrah, Alicante
Alcohol 12.5%
Importer O'Briens
Stockist O'Briens

Price about £8 (€10)

SOUTH

James Herrick Millia Passum Syrah
Vin de Pays d'Oc 1998

Down in the Languedoc, Australian winemaker James Herrick turns out some scrumptious wines, packed with local character. This dense, dark beauty has the whiff of herbs and rubber so typical of Syrah in the south of France, and its intense, spicy flavours are tantalisingly slow to fade.

Grape Syrah
Alcohol 13%
Importer Oddbins
Stockist Oddbins

Price about £9 (€11.45)

SOUTH

**Château Pech-Latt Corbières
1999**

With its aromas of ripe berry fruits and its full-on flavours, this organic southern red makes for very attractive, uncomplicated drinking. Although there's a nice twist of pepper mid-palate, the overall effect is chocolatey-smooth. Indeed, you'll even taste a slick of chocolate in the finish.

Grapes Carignan, Grenache
Alcohol 13%
Importer Woodford Bourne
Stockists selected SuperValus · Molloys · Pettitts in southeast +++

Price £9-£10 (€11.45-€12.70)

FRANCE

SOUTH

FRANCE

Château de Flaugergues, Coteaux du Languedoc La Méjanelle 1997

As you might guess from its tall, heavy bottle, this is a wine with serious pretensions, aged in oak until its ripe, concentrated fruit has developed beautifully mature, figgy overtones with a smoky, slightly tarry edge. Although it costs a few pounds more than many wines from the south of France, it has real staying power and intrigue. Definitely worth sampling.

Grapes Mourvèdre, Syrah, Grenache
Alcohol 13%
Importer Dunnes Stores
Stockists Dunnes Stores leading outlets

Price about £11 (€13.95)

SOUTH

Domaine Rimbert Le Mas au Schiste
Saint-Chinian 1999

Here is an offering for anybody who's curious to discover how far some of the committed, small growers in the Languedoc have progressed along the road towards sophisticated, deeply satisfying wines. Scented with blackberries, black cherries, caramel, spice and the merest whiff of rubber, this is a smooth, polished effort with a flick of tannic grip in the tail.

Grapes Carignan, Syrah, Grenache, Cinsault, Mourvèdre
Alcohol 14%
Importer Bubble Brothers
Stockist Bubble Brothers, Dún Laoghaire & Cork

Price about £13 (€16.50)

**Rapsani Reserve
Epilegmenos, Tsantalis 1996**

From the same stable as the easy-going Nemea (see page 103) comes this slightly richer wine - a bit more mature but smacking of youthful vigour. Fragrant as a Christmas cake, it has spicy, plummy fruit, really lively acidity and supple tannins that all fuse in a firm, dry finish. Food is a must with this. It's especially delicious with something fatty, like pork.

Grapes Xinomavro, Stavroto, Krassato
Alcohol 12.5%
Importer Hellenic Marketing
Stockist Dunnes Stores

Price about £8.50 (€10.80)

Canaletto Primitivo, Puglia
Casa Girelli 1999

ITALY

Primitivo, Zinfandel's twin grape from southern Italy, is beginning to star in its own right. Here's a modestly priced example with a fleshy texture and robust flavours - ripe, dark berries and that tiny touch of rubber that is so reminiscent of daredevil Italian drivers. It's forthright, even slightly rustic - and that comes as a relief in these polished times.

Grape Primitivo
Alcohol 13.5%
Importer James Adams
Stockists widely available

Price about £7 (€8.90)

ITALY

Primitivo Salento
Pasqua 1999

Made from the fruit of old vines, this smooth, modern version of Primitivo is rather like an Apulian country lad sporting Armani shades and driving a Maserati. Chock full of mulberry and fig flavours with that southern whiff of rubber, it has a nice juicy bite in the middle and a long, pleasantly chewy mocha finish.

Grape Primitivo
Alcohol 13%
Importer Woodford Bourne
Stockists selected SuperValus · selected Cheers and Next-Door outlets · Molloys · Mitchells, Kildare St & Glasthule · Fine Wines, Limerick · O'Donovans, Cork +

Price £7.50-£8 (€9.50-€10)

A Mano Primitivo
Puglia 2000

ITALY

The third member of our Primitivo trio is another hip, modern smoothie. From American winemaker-turned-Apulian-winery-owner Mark Shannon, it avoids the tarry, rubbery excess that this grape can exhibit in clumsy hands. Instead, it's rich and succulent with a really long, spicy finish. The bottle's pretty smart, too.

Grape Primitivo
Alcohol 13.5%
Importer irelandonwine.com
Stockist irelandonwine.com

Price £8-£8.50 (€10-€10.80)

ITALY

**Tesco Chianti Classico Riserva
1997**

Over the past couple of years, the Chianti Riserva has been one of Tesco's most consistently appealing own-label wines. This one from the excellent 1997 vintage has sweet, black fruits and smoky allure with an assertive, spicy finish. It's strikingly high in acidity, though. Turn this into a bonus by drinking it with something fatty, like pork or duck.

Grape Sangiovese
Alcohol 13%
Importer Tesco
Stockist Tesco

Price £8-£8.50 (€10-€10.80)

ITALY

**Elorina Villa Dorata Eloro Rosso
1998**

There's been a lot of excitement recently about rich, southern-Italian reds - but to my mind this Sicilian knocks many of its clumsier cousins from the heel-and-toe areas into a bandit's hat. Smooth, lively and polished with subtle spicy length, it has bags of personality seeping through in the ripe, black-cherry flavours of the warm south.

Grape Nero d'Avola
Alcohol 12.5%
Importer Findlater
Stockists Sweeneys, Dorset St · Higgins, Clonskeagh · Jus de Vine, Portmarnock · Wine Bottle, Dunshaughlin · Fahys, Ballina · Vineyard, Galway +

Price £8-£8.50 (€10-€10.80)

Cappello di Prete
Salento Rosso, Candido 1997

Candido's Salice Salentino is a huge success in Ireland, but it's worth trading up one level to savour the richer, more mature big brother. Deep and dark, with port-like overtones of raisins, dates and figs, it was memorably described by an *Irish Times* reader as "a restrained extravagance of a red, with a long and satisfying finish that ends with a smile". I can't say better.

Grapes Negroamaro
Alcohol 13%
Importer Findlater
Stockists Raheny Wine Cellar · Kelly's, Artane · Mortons, Ranelagh · Deveney's, Dundrum · Loughnane's Food Hall, Galway · Octavius, Sligo +

Price about £8.50 (€10.80)

ITALY

Cantina Zaccagnini, il vino dal tralcetto
Montepulciano d'Abruzzo 1998

If you find southern Italian reds a tad over-endowed with porty richness, reach for this brilliantly harmonious wine from middle Italy instead. Nicknamed Twiggy (because the bottle comes with a bit of vine twig tied around its neck), it balances soft, plummy fruit with juicy, sour cherry bite and tannic grip in perfect proportions. An irresistible Italian all-rounder.

Grape Montepulciano
Alcohol 12.5%
Importer J & T Davy
Stockists Searsons, Monkstown · Layden Wines, Liffey St · Michael's Wines, Mount Merrion · De Vine Wine Shop, Castleknock · Wicklow Wine Co. · O'Donovans, Cork ++

Price about £9.50 (€12)

Cantina Zaccagnini
il vino "dal tralcetto"
montepulciano d'Abruzzo
denominazione d'origine controllata
imbottigliato all'origine dall'Az. Agricola Cirio Zaccagnini s.a.s
C. da Pozzo - Bolognano Pe - Italy
750 ml ℮   12,5 % vol.

Masi Campofiorin Ripasso
Rosso del Veronese 1997

The clever *ripasso* technique, which involves refermenting light, fruity Valpolicella on the lees of concentrated Amarone, produces a wine half-way in style between the two. Campofiorin, the pioneer, is a meaty and intriguing example infused with pepper, warm-spice, earthy tones and some of Amarone's raisiny richness - along with the traditional bitter-sweet finale.

Grapes Corvina, Rondinella, Molinara
Alcohol 13%
Importer Grants of Ireland
Stockists Tesco · Superquinn and many independent off-licences

Price £10.50–£11 (€13.35–€13.95)

ITALY

Regaleali Rosso
Tasca d'Almerita 1999

We don't normally think of Sicily as a source of sophisticated wines, but this suave and luxuriously textured red is a reminder that maybe we should. From the Tasca family, top-rated producers, it has sweet, concentrated flavours of prunes and vanilla supported by ripe tannins. Worth the money.

Grapes Nero d'Avola, Perricone
Alcohol 12.5%
Importer Select Wines of Italy
Stockists McCabes, Blackrock · Dunne & Crescenzi, South Frederick St · Wicklow Wine Co. · Wine Centre, Kilkenny · McCambridges, Galway · Bradleys, Cork +

Price about £11 (€13.95)

ITALY

La Gavina, Cabernet Sauvignon Toscana Cecchi 1997

If your view of Tuscan wines has been skewed by too many thin and tart Chiantis, consider a brief switch in allegiance from Sangiovese to Cabernet. Smoky on the nose, velvety on the palate with lingering flavours of black cherries and dates, this a quintessentially Italian Cabernet - a SuperTuscan at a more than reasonable price.

Grape Cabernet Sauvignon
Alcohol 13%
Importer Dunnes Stores
Stockists Dunnes Stores leading outlets

Price £11.50-£12 (€14.60-€15.25)

**Ripassa Valpolicella Classico Superiore
Zenato 1998**

ITALY

This *ripasso* wine takes sumptuousness to mouth-watering extremes. Made by Alberto Zenato - one of the most exciting winemakers to feature in this book (see also pages 25 and 167) - it has almost New World lushness, with concentrated black fruits, a suggestion of black chocolate and the supplest of tannins delivering smooth staying power.

Grapes Corvina, Molinara, Rondinella
Alcohol 13%
Importer J & T Davy
Stockists Searsons, Monkstown · On the Grapevine, Dalkey · Murtagh's, Enniskerry · Ryan Vine, Navan · Wine Centre, Kilkenny · Vineyard, Galway ++

Price about £13 (€16.50)

ITALY

Airone Monferrato
Michele Chiarlo 1997

Leading Piedmont producer Michele Chiarlo shows his mettle with this seriously tempting, big-boned wine. All the northern-Italian elements you'd expect - ripe cherry flavours with a palate-awakening bite of acidity and brooding, chewy tannins - fuse in glorious harmony. Treat it to substantial food.

Grapes Barbera, Nebbiolo, Cabernet Sauvignon
Alcohol 13%
Importer Taserra
Stockists Carvills, Camden St · Raheny Wine Cellar · Vintry, Rathgar · Old Stand, Mullingar · Al Vinos, Athlone · Shannon Knights, Shannon +

Price £13-£14 (€16.50-€17.80)

Nipozzano Chianti Rufina Riserva
Frescobaldi 1997

I've had a weakness for this sensuous but restrained Tuscan for a long time. There's a faint earthiness, an edge of great authenticity, to its cherry fruit and subtle spice. Like a cashmere wrap, the 1997 feels luxurious and softly enveloping as ever, yet there's underlying firmness and length. A great buy for a stylish dinner, in or out.

Grape Sangiovese
Alcohol 12.5%
Importer Allied Drinks
Stockists De Vine Wine Shop, Castleknock · SuperValu, Malahide · Mill Wine Cellar, Maynooth · Terrys, Limerick · Dalys, Boyle · Galvins, Cork +

Price about £13.50 (€17)

ITALY

Selvapiana Chianti Rufina Riserva 1997

From a leading Chianti estate in an excellent vintage, this is a real Tuscan beauty. Exotically dark and rich with hints of maraschino cherries, dates and prunes, its sumptuous fruit is countered by lively acidity and smooth, fine-grained tannins. The result? A glorious wine whose intense, complex flavours ebb in a slow, majestic finish. Superb.

Grape Sangiovese
Alcohol 14%
Importer Karwig Wines
Stockists Karwigs, Carrigaline · selected Molloys outlets · Il Primo, Montague St +++

Price £17–£18 (€21.60–€22.90)

Zenato Amarone della Valpolicella Classico Veneto 1997

The third wine in this book from the talented Veneto producer Alberto Zenato (see also pages 25 and 163) is the most impressive of all. Fabulously dark and rich, this new-wave Amarone cloaks its massive body in a smooth overcoat of sweet, concentrated fruit and ripe, manageable tannins. I'd settle into this by the fire, late on a winter's night, with a hunk of Parmesan - and feel like a princess.

Grapes Corvina, Molinara, Rondinella
Alcohol 14%
Importer J & T Davy
Stockists Searsons, Monkstown · Vintry, Rathgar · DeVine Wine Shop, Castleknock · Ryan Vine, Navan · Wicklow Wine Co. · DeVine Wines, Letterkenny +

Price £25-£26 (€31.75-€33)

PORTUGAL

J. P. Tinto Regional, Terras do Sado
J. P. Vinhos 1996

Not to be confused with the basic and much lighter J. P. red,
the oak-aged Regional delivers oodles more pleasure for about
an extra £2. Aromas of figs, dates, coffee and other dark
delights with a slightly earthy edge carry through powerfully on
the palate, leading to a rich finish with plenty of grip. A winner
at the price.

Grape Periquita
Alcohol 13%
Importer T. P. Reynolds
Stockists widely available

Price about £6 (€7.60)

Tinto da Anfora, Vinho Regional Alentejano
J. P. Vinhos 1998

Look at that list of grapes and you'll see exactly why Portugal
can lay claim to original, distinctive wines. A hint of earthiness
adds interest to softly enveloping, dark fruits shot through with
vanilla and sweet gentle spice. Velvety Anfora is a good alternative
to Rioja at a budget price, and it ages well, too.

Grapes Periquita, Alfrocheiro, Trincadeira, Aragonez, Moreto
Alcohol 13%
Importer T. P. Reynolds
Stockists SuperValus · Centras · Roches Stores

Price about £9 (€11.45)

PORTUGAL

D'Avillez, Vinho Regional Alentejo
J M da Fonseca 1996/1997

If you feel in the mood for a red wine that's deliciously different and stylish too, look out for this one from Portugal's up-
and-coming Alentejo region. It has soft, herb-tinged blackberry
fruit in a smooth vanilla wrap, perky acidity and ripe tannins in
just the right proportions. With its emphatically dry finish, it
definitely needs food.

Grapes Trincadeira, Aragonez, Tinta Francesa
Alcohol 13%
Importer Gilbeys
Stockists Redmonds, Ranelagh · Pettitts in southeast +

Price £9.50-£10 (€12-€12.70)

Duas Quintas Douro
Ramos-Pinto 1997

PORTUGAL

A reminder that Portugal's great port region, the Douro, is focusing increasingly on high-quality, red table wines. This is a smooth, fleshy middleweight - a well-integrated wine whose rich, plummy fruit is infused with vanilla and warm spice, with a subtle touch of earthiness. Supple tannins and a moreish finish add to its appeal.

Grapes Tinta Roriz, Touriga Nacional
Alcohol 12.5%
Importer J & T Davy
Stockists Searsons, Monkstown · McCabes, Blackrock & Foxrock · Michael's Wines, Mount Merrion · Wicklow Wine Co. · DeVine Wines, Letterkenny +

Price £10-£11 (€12-70-€14)

SPAIN

Marques de Aragón Old Vine Garnacha
Calatayud 1999

A wine to guzzle greedily rather than sip demurely. This big, warming, rustic gobsmacker of a red, made from the small, concentrated grapes of 60-year-old vines, has oodles of smooth, chocolatey richness, juicy acidity and a very respectable savoury finish. Great for mid-week cheer.

Grape Garnacha
Alcohol 13.5%
Importer J & T Davy
Stockists Searsons, Monkstown · Michael's Wines, Mount Merrion · DeVine Wine Shop, Castleknock · Country Choice, Nenagh · DeVine Wines, Letterkenny +

Price about £8 (€10)

SPAIN

Raimat Abadia, Costers del Segre
1998

With its silky texture and layers of subtle interest, this smooth, elegant red deserves its devoted following. There's a firm backbone beneath the sumptuously mature, spicy fruit, contributing depth of flavour and a nice savoury finale. Smart enough for a dinner party - but don't feel you have to wait for that.

Grapes Cabernet Sauvignon, Merlot, Tempranillo
Alcohol 13%
Importer Grants of Ireland
Stockists selected SuperValus · Redmonds, Ranelagh · Kielys, Mount Merrion · Sweeneys, Dorset St & Fairview · Joyces, Knocknacarra ++

Price about £9.50 (€12)

SPAIN

Mas Collet, Tarragona
Capçanes 1999

This is one of those soulful wines that makes you want to jump for joy - just because it tastes so pure, so 'real', in a world invaded by confected, characterless nonentities. Salute the new Spain! Made from the fruit of old vines by a reinvented co-op with vision, it has layer upon layer of vibrant flavour and a long, firm finish. The bottle just empties itself . . .

Grapes Garnacha, Tempranillo, Cariñena, Cabernet Sauvignon
Alcohol 13.5%
Importer James Nicholson
Stockists James Nicholson Direct · Michael's Wines, Mount Merrion · Ryan Vine, Navan · Cuisine de Vendange, Naas · Wicklow Wine Co. · Wine Centre, Kilkenny +

Price £9.50-£10 (€12-€12.70)

Mas Collet
1999

Tarragona
Zona Falset
Denominación de Origen

Elaborado y Embotellado por Celler de Capçanes SCCRL
N.E. 2161/T Spain
75cl. 13,5%vol

Gazur, Ribera del Duero
Telmo Rodriguez 1999

An exciting offering from the young Turk who's shaking up vineyards and cellars all over Spain - squeezing out plumper, riper wines. Smoky and exotically fruity with a satisfying, chewy finish, this is by far the richest, tastiest red from swanky Ribera del Duero that I've come across at this price. As always with Rodriguez, the bottle is as smart as the wine.

Grapes Tinto del Pais
Alcohol 13.5%
Importer Approach Trade Ireland
Stockists Mitchells, Kildare St & Glasthule · Michael's Wines, Mount Merrion · On the Grapevine, Dalkey · Wicklow Wine Co. · Karwig Wines, Carrigaline · McCambridges, Galway +

Price £9.50-£10 (€12-€12.70)

SPAIN

Albet i Noya Lignum
Penedès 1999

The aristocratic cousin of Can Vendrell (page 113) is a very smart organic red from Josep Maria Albet, one of Catalonia's most gifted new-wave winemakers. Aromas of spiced plums and freshly turned earth jump out of the glass; layers of spicy intensity unfold stirringly on the palate and seem to stay for minutes. Super stuff.

Grapes Garnacha, Cariñena, Cabernet Sauvignon
Alcohol 13%
Importer Mary Pawle
Stockists Good Food Store, Pembroke Lane · Sweeneys, Dorset St · Egan's Food Hall, Drogheda · Quay Co-op, Cork · Pantry, Kenmare · Connemara Hamper, Clifden +

Price about £10 (€12.70)

**Palacio de la Vega Tempranillo Reserva
Navarra 1996**

A classic Spanish marriage of sweet, spicy fruit and ripe but meaty tannins, this is a nicely mature wine with beautifully integrated, subtle flavours, lovely balance and a long, engaging finish. Its younger brother, the basic Tempranillo, though more straightforward, is a good buy too for a couple of pounds less.

Grape Tempranillo
Alcohol 12.5%
Importer Irish Distillers
Stockists Vintry, Rathgar · Mill Wine Cellar, Maynooth · Wine World, Waterford · Pettitts in southeast ++

Price £10-£11 (€12.70-€13.95)

SPAIN

Condado de Haza, Ribera del Duero
Alejandro Fernandez 1998

The sibling of Spain's legendary Pesquera has the same rippling muscles and brooding presence (and, according to the man who makes them both, may soon outstrip the more famous wine in terms of sheer panache). With aromas of polished leather and opulent fruit, it's big, brawny and beautifully complex - an extrovert oozing personality. Don't think of serving it without meat.

Grape Tinto del Pais
Alcohol 13%
Importer J & T Davy
Stockists Searsons, Monkstown · Vaughan Johnsons, Temple Bar · Berry Bros, Harry St · Cheers-Gibneys, Malahide · Egans, Drogheda · Wicklow Wine Co. ++

Price about £16 (€20.30)

Les Terrasses, Priorat
Alvaro Palacios 1998/1999

From the chap who vowed, with his top wine L'Ermita, to give Spain a Château Pétrus, this stunningly concentrated, exquisitely balanced and more affordable rendering is voluptuous without being overwhelming. Priorato, the new viticultural Eden in the northeast, and the young perfectionistic Palacios make a potent combination.

Grapes Garnacha, Cariñena, Cabernet Sauvignon
Alcohol 13.7%
Importer Approach Trade Ireland
Stockists Mitchells, Kildare St & Glasthule · Gourmet Gallery, Rathmines · On the Grapevine, Dalkey · Sky and the Ground, Wexford · Karwig Wines, Carrigaline · Egans, Liscannor +

Price about £17 (€21.60)

ARGENTINA

Trapiche Oak Cask Malbec
Mendoza 1998

Judging by sales, a lot of people view this old favourite as the
Jacob's Cream Cracker of Malbecs in Ireland - the original and
best. I can't say I blame them. It's a big, rich mouthful, as laden
with Christmas spices as mulled wine and, though supple, has
an agreeably chewy core.

Grape Malbec
Alcohol 13.5%
Importer Comans
Stockists widely available

Price £8-£8.50 (€10-€10.80)

TRAPICHE
Malbec
OAK CASK
1998

13.5% Vol.   75 CL ℮

Norton Malbec
Mendoza 2000

Swiss-owned Norton is widely regarded as one of Argentina's most progressive producers. This modern-style Malbec, full, rich and round, backs up that theory with conviction. Vigorous aromas of blackberries and spice are confirmed in a punchy palate with excellent length. All that's missing is a plate of beef.

Grape Malbec
Alcohol 13%
Importers Oddbins · James Nicholson
Stockists Oddbins · James Nicholson Direct · Cheers-Gibneys, Malahide · Redmonds, Ranelagh · Egans, Drogheda · Next-Door, Wexford +

Price about £8.50 (€10.80)

Weinert Pedro de Castillo Malbec
Mendoza 1999/2000

With its fragrant perfume of damsons, loganberries and vanilla, its ultra-soft tannins and terrific balancing acidity, this Malbec from a small, pedigree producer has real elegance and class. Not quite light enough to qualify as a 'lighter red', it's a soft and enveloping middleweight.

Grapes Malbec
Alcohol 12.5%
Importer Woodford Bourne
Stockists Mitchells, Kildare St & Glasthule · Deveneys, Dundrum · Jus de Vine, Portmarnock · Kitchen, Portlaoise · Vineyard, Galway +

Price about £10 (€12.70)

ARGENTINA

Navarra Correas Colección Privada
Altos del Rio Mendoza 1997

Although its lush blackberry aromas are exactly what you'd expect of an Argentine red, there's a refinement of flavour, a lightness of touch, which puts this liquorice-edged beauty closer to Bordeaux. Don't pass the black frosted bottle by. It deserves to be much better known.

Grape Cabernet Sauvignon, Merlot
Alcohol 12.7%
Importer Gilbeys
Stockists Tesco · Superquinn · Ardkeen, Waterford · Vineyard, Galway ++

Price £10-£11 (€12.70-€13.95)

ARGENTINA

Arnaldo B. Etchart Vino Fino Tinto Cafayate 1998

The Etchart flagship wine needs a couple of years to soften, so buy it now to tuck away. Lusciously sweet blackberries and damsons with a caramel topping dominate the nose; the mocha-toned palate is intensely spicy and still quite tannic, but all those flavours will gradually meld into a concentrated, impressive wine.

Grapes Malbec, Cabernet Sauvignon
Alcohol 13.5%
Importer Irish Distillers
Stockists selected Superquinns · O'Briens · McHughs, Kilbarrack · Egans, Drogheda · Pettitts in southeast · Lynchs, Glanmire ++

Price about £11 (€13.95)

ARNALDO B. ETCHART
VINO FINO TINTO
CAFAYATE
1998

13.5% VOL.   PRODUCE OF ARGENTINA   75 cl

Wakefield Cabernet Sauvignon
Clare Valley 1999

Here you have Australian Cabernet at its most user-friendly. Laden with blackberry and blackcurrant flavours, it's chocolate-rich, layered with spice and that hint of eucalyptus that always reminds me of gum trees. Like its pale Riesling sister (see page 35), this Wakefield mainstay seems to get better and better.

AUSTRALIA

Grape Cabernet Sauvignon
Alcohol 14.5%
Importer Koala Wines
Stockists Superquinn · SuperValus · Centras · Roches Stores · Pettitts in southeast ++

Price about £9 (€11.45)

AUSTRALIA

**Tesco McLaren Vale Shiraz
1998**

If you're into buttoned-up restraint, stop reading now. But if you're tempted to try the extravagantly voluptuous McLaren Vale style of Shiraz without extravagant outlay, seek out this well-made representative. Black fruits, caramel, tobacco, spice, black pepper, chocolate ... they're all there in lavish abundance.

Grape Shiraz
Alcohol 13%
Importer Tesco
Stockist Tesco

Price about £9 (€11.45)

**Peter Lehmann The Barossa Shiraz
1999**

Without the efforts of Peter Lehmann, who helped to save countless acres of old vines, the Barossa Valley wouldn't be identified today as the home of full-blooded, meaty Australian Shiraz. This is the benchmark - dark and rich, with masses of sweet, concentrated fruit, clove spice and tannic thrust. A real winter warmer.

Grape Shiraz
Alcohol 14%
Importer Comans
Stockists Superquinn · many SuperValus · many Centras · Roches Stores · Molloys · O'Donovans, Cork +++

Price £9-£10 (€11.45-€12.70)

AUSTRALIA

**Tesco Coonawarra Cabernet Sauvignon
1997**

I'd love to put this tall, handsome bottle on the dinner table of everybody who's ever complained that Australian reds are too sweet and fruity and obvious. From the heartland of classy Cabernet, this is a super wine with reminders of meat juice, minerals and herbs, and enough lively acidity to keep perking up the palate. It's both supple and subtle. Hooray!

Grape Cabernet Sauvignon
Alcohol 12.5%
Importer Tesco
Stockist Tesco

Price about £9.50 (€12)

**Penfolds Koonunga Hill Shiraz-Cabernet Sauvignon
South Australia 1998**

My first taste of this came after a long winter walk on Dún
Laoghaire pier, and I still think of it as a cheerful, warming life-
saver. Plenty of lovely ripe berry flavours and a good whack of
vanilla and spicy oak come together smoothly in a soft, round
red with immediate appeal.

Grapes Shiraz, Cabernet Sauvignon
Alcohol 14%
Importer Findlater
Stockists widely available

Price about £10 (€12.70)

AUSTRALIA

AUSTRALIA

Chateau Tahbilk Shiraz
Victoria 1997

Victoria delivers Shiraz with a difference - medium-bodied and finely tuned, not turbo-charged. Slightly feral on the nose, peppery and vigorous on the palate, the remarkable Tahbilk keeps well for anything from 10 to 20 years from the date of vintage. Few red wines at this price have such cellaring potential. (Château Tahbilk Marsanne features on page 68.)

Grape Shiraz
Alcohol 13.5%
Importer Comans
Stockists selected SuperValus · Bourkes, Cabinteely · Martha's Vineyard, Rathfarnham · Jus de Vine, Portmarnock · Mill Wine Cellar, Maynooth · O'Donovans, Cork +

Price about £10 (€12.70)

Wynns Coonawarra Estate Cabernet-Shiraz-Merlot 1996

Coonawarra is supposed to be synonymous with stylish wines. Not all deliver as rewardingly as this one, nor at such a fair price. Aromas of black fruit gums and mint follow through on the palate with a delicious explosion of spice - but what you'll remember most are the silky texture and juicy length. (Wynns Coonawarra Riesling features on page 34.)

Grapes Cabernet Sauvignon, Shiraz, Merlot
Alcohol 13.5%
Importer Findlater
Stockists Redmonds, Ranelagh · Deveneys, SCR · Londis, Malahide · SuperValu, Drogheda · Ashford Food & Wines, Co. Wicklow +

Price £11-£11.50 (€13.95-€14.60)

AUSTRALIA

AUSTRALIA

Omrah Shiraz, Western Australia-McLaren Vale Plantagenet 1999

With a mix of grapes from warm McLaren Vale and cool Western Australia, this relatively restrained Shiraz has the best of both worlds. Although it has rich aromas with a mint chocolate and caramel overlay, it's delightfully vivacious and supple, with a long, satisfying finish.

Grape Shiraz
Alcohol 13.5%
Importer irelandonwine.com
Stockist irelandonwine.com

Price about £11.50 (€14.60)

D'Arenberg The Twentyeight Road Mourvèdre McLaren Vale 1998

Pure Mourvèdre can make a wild beast of a wine, but fastidious D'Arenberg (see also pages 202 and 245) has tamed its animal character without destroying its soul. With overtones of blackberries, rubber, herbs and fresh earth, this spunky South Australian is multi-layered and irrepressibly lively.

Grape Mourvèdre
Alcohol 14%
Importer Taserra
Stockists Vintry, Rathgar · McCabes, Blackrock & Foxrock · McHughs, Kilbarrack · Blessings, Cavan · Al Vino's, Athlone · Wine Cellar, Portlaoise +

Price £13-£14 (€16.50-€17.75)

AUSTRALIA

Rothbury Estate Brokenback Shiraz
Hunter Valley 1998

Australia's Hunter Valley is noted for medium-bodied Shiraz with distinctive overtones of polished leather and cracked pepper. This classic example is strikingly perky on the palate. Dark red fruit flavours are lifted by a peppery punch, leading into a long, smooth, vanilla finish.

Grape Shiraz
Alcohol 13%
Importer Cassidy
Stockists Berry Bros, Harry St · McHughs, Kilbarrack · Kellys, Clontarf · Cheers-Wicklow Arms, Delgany · Wicklow Wine Co. · Macs, Limerick +

Price about £14 (€17.75)

Coldstream Hills Pinot Noir
Yarra Valley 1999

Subtlety and delicacy? Er, no. This Pinot Noir, made by leading Aussie man-about-wine James Halliday, has been on a body-building course. There's a smoky, oaky framework to its rich plum and cherry fruit, but all that swagger is balanced by the juicy acidity Burgundy fans expect.

Grape Pinot Noir
Alcohol 13.5%
Importer Findlater
Stockists O'Briens · Kellys, Artane · Berrys, Harry St · McCabes, Blackrock & Foxrock · Cana Wines, Mullingar · Vineyard, Galway ++

Price £14-£15 (€17.75-€19)

AUSTRALIA

Tatachilla Clarendon Vineyard Merlot
McLaren Vale 1998

Supposing it's a freezing evening and you crave a big, thermal red? Although this opulent Australian blockbuster is dense and fairly alcoholic, it's terrifically vigorous on the palate, with smooth, lingering flavours of dark berries, mocha and spice.

Grape Merlot
Alcohol 14%
Importer O'Briens
Stockist O'Briens

Price about £15 (€19)

Geoff Merrill Cabernet Sauvignon Reserve
South Australia 1995

Because Merrill's reserve wines are made to last, they have several years of maturity in their favour before being released - a virtue that is all too rare these days. The result? Really well-integrated flavours and a sort of suave elegance. Suggestions of leather and mint sit on a plump blackcurrant base, making this almost like a modern Bordeaux. Subtle and lingering.

Grape Cabernet Sauvignon
Alcohol 13%
Importer Comans
Stockists Redmonds, Ranelagh · Higgins, Clonskeagh · Deveneys, Dundrum · Raheny Wine Cellar · Londis, Malahide · Cheers-Wicklow Arms, Delgany +

Price about £15 (€19)

AUSTRALIA

Greg Norman Estates Coonawarra Cabernet-Merlot 1998

With Greg's shark symbol on the label, you'd be forgiven for thinking this must be the overpriced by-product of a big Mildara Blass marketing deal. Not so. As a key investor in a premium vineyard, the wine-loving golfer is into quality. This is a very well-made wine from Australia's classiest Cabernet region - silky, complex and rewarding.

Grapes Cabernet, Merlot
Alcohol 13%
Importer Cassidy
Stockists selected Superquinns · Berry Bros, Harry St · Cheers-Gibneys, Malahide · Ardkeen, Waterford · Scallys, Blackrock, Cork +

Price about £16 (€20.30)

AUSTRALIA

Château Reynella Basket-Pressed Shiraz
McLaren Vale 1998

Velvety and richly luxurious, this turkey-friendly Shiraz is a
perennial recommendation for Christmas dinner - and I've yet
to meet anybody who doesn't enjoy it. But why wait for
Christmas? With lush overtones of blackberries, chocolate and
warming spice, soft tannins and superb length, it's a plushy year-
round treat.

Grape Shiraz
Alcohol 14%
Importer Allied Drinks
Stockists Redmonds, Ranelagh · De Vine Wine Shop,
Castleknock · Cheers-Gibneys, Malahide · Noble Rot, Navan ·
Old Stand, Mullingar · Galvins, Cork +

Price £16-£17 (€20.30-€21.60)

AUSTRALIA

Rosemount GSM
McLaren Vale 1997

If you like your red wines turbo-charged and as extrovert as
Paul Hogan, this dramatic blend is for you. With lashings of dark
berry fruit, liberal spice and a great dollop of vanilla cushioning
a chewy core, it's an opulent, high-alcohol biggie. Keep it for a
few years if you can.

Grapes Grenache, Syrah, Mourvèdre
Alcohol 14.5%
Importer Grants of Ireland
Stockists selected O'Briens outlets · Redmonds, Ranelagh ·
Kellys, Artane · Sweeneys, Dorset St · Mill, Maynooth · Egans,
Drogheda +

Price about £17 (€21.60)

1997
G S M
McLAREN VALE · GRENACHE SYRAH MOURVÈDRE

ROSEMOUNT

St Hallett Old Block Shiraz
Barossa Valley 1996/1997

Classic Barossa Shiraz under £20 doesn't get much better than
this one, made from the tiny grapes of 70-to-100-year-old vines
using traditional methods. Big aromas of ripe berries, liquorice
and eucalyptus give way to a peppery attack, then a subtle
touch of chocolate mid-palate. With excellent acidity and a
long, firm finish, it will live happily for another 10 years at least.

Grape Shiraz
Alcohol 13.5%/14%
Importer O'Briens
Stockists O'Briens · some remaining stock may also be in
Dunnes Stores

Price about £20 (€25.40)

AUSTRALIA

D'Arenberg The Coppermine Road Cabernet Sauvignon, McLaren Vale 1998

I'll admit, it: I've spat out 20 times more Cabernets from McLaren Vale than I've enjoyed. They're often just too sweet and rich. This, however, is a magnificent exception - a polished star that delivers all the region's lavishness without going OTT. Sit back and savour lovely, spicy concentration with a long mocha finish. (More D'Arenberg delights are on pages 193 and 245.)

Grape Cabernet Sauvignon
Alcohol 14%
Importer Taserra
Stockists Carvills, Camden St · Vintry, Rathgar · Raheny Wine Cellar · Shannon Knights, Shannon · Macs, Limerick · Loughnane's, Loughrea +

Price £22-£24 (€27.95-€30.50)

CHILE

Santa Ines Cabernet Sauvignon
Maipo Valley 1999/2000

The switched-on De Martino family (who also bottle under their own name) have made significant improvements in both vineyards and cellar since 1990 - resulting in flavourful, good value wines. This basic Cabernet, blackcurranty and herbal, is extremely lively on the palate with a firm, savoury finish. A Chilean frontrunner at the price. (The Sauvignon Blanc is recommended on page 40.)

Grapes Cabernet Sauvignon, Carmenère
Alcohol 13%
Importer Mackenway
Stockists Molloys · selected Cheers Take-Home outlets · Listons, Camden St · Brackens, Glasnevin · Mortons, Ranelagh · C&T, Skerries ++

Price about £7 (€8.90)

CHILE

Carmen Merlot
Central Valley 2000

For quality and consistency right across its range, one Chilean winery that really stands out is Carmen, the showcase baby sister of Santa Rita. While the reserva wines are especially impressive (the Reserve Sauvignon is on page 41), this basic Merlot is a super mid-week or party buy - densely flavoured and peppery with overtones of mint.

Grape Merlot
Alcohol 13.5%
Importer Edward Dillon
Stockists widely available

Price £7-£7.50 (€8.90-9.50)

Tesco Chilean Merlot Reserve
Curicó 1999

A Frenchman into whose hand I thrust a glass of this pro-
nounced it "so good even French people could enjoy it". Wow!
Smooth and intense with a velvety texture and plenty of spicy
thrust, it's made for Tesco by the widely acclaimed producer
Valdivieso. Great drinking for the money.

Grape Merlot
Alcohol 13%
Importer Tesco
Stockist Tesco

Price about £7.50 (€9.50)

CHILE

**Casillero del Diablo Cabernet Sauvignon
Maipo, Concha y Toro 2000**

If I were rationed to one Chilean Cabernet for the rest of my
life (perish the thought), it might well be this because it's far
from one-dimensional. Typical aromas of ripe blackcurrants
and cassis with a dash of herbs give way to surprisingly
savoury, peppery flavours, and though the wine is smooth as
can be, the finish has plenty of firm grip.

Grape Cabernet Sauvignon
Alcohol 13.5%
Importer Findlater
Stockists widely available

Price about £8 (€10)

Castillo de Molina Cabernet Sauvignon Reserva Lontue 1999

Sniff all that concentrated cassis and you think: just another run-of-the-mill Chilean Cabernet. But this is way better than run-of-the-mill, with a firm structure and a long, meaty finish. Incidentally, the Castillo de Molina label belongs to Viña San Pedro, whose wines are in Dunnes Stores. (The San Pedro Sauvignon features on page 39.)

Grapes Cabernet Sauvignon
Alcohol 12.5%
Importer Cassidy
Stockists Londis outlets · Berry Bros, Harry St · McCabes, Blackrock & Foxrock · Bradys, Shankill · Cheers-Wicklow Arms, Delgany · Ashford Food & Wine, Co. Wicklow ++

Price £9-£10 (€11.45-€12.70)

CHILE

**Mont Gras Quatro Reserva
Colchagua 1999**

Four grapes and a kiss of French oak make for a complex, elegant Chilean whose flavours are beautifully knitted together. Although not short of intense, ripe fruit, this stylish blend comes across as admirably light-footed and vibrant, with super spicy length.

Grapes Cabernet Sauvignon, Merlot, Carmenère, Malbec
Alcohol 13%
Importer Maxxium
Stockists SuperValus · Centras · Roches Stores · selected Tescos · O'Briens ++

Price about £10 (€12.70)

Cousino-Macul Antiguas Reservas
Cabernet Sauvignon, Maipo 1998

There are any number of souped up 'premium' Chileans on the market - too concentrated, too oaky, trying too damned hard. And there's this - a quiet, unswaggering presence getting it right for years. Made from 80-year-old vines, it marries Old World subtlety (look out for Bordeaux overtones of leather and meat juice) with New World drinkability. Very distinctive.

Grape Cabernet Sauvignon
Alcohol 12.5%
Importer Woodford Bourne
Stockists selected SuperValus · selected Centras · Roches Stores · selected Superquinns · Deveneys group ·Vineyard, Galway · Fine Wines, Limerick · Kitchen, Portlaoise +

Price about £10 (€12.70)

CHILE

**Santa Rita Carmenère Reserva
Rapel 1999**

Carmenère is Chile's answer to Argentina's Malbec - a speciality grape. Whereas some examples are just too luscious for their own good, this one, though supple, veers towards the meaty end of the spectrum. It's pleasantly complex, too - not just the usual Carmenére basket of chocolate-coated ripe black fruits.

Grapes Carmenère, Cabernet Sauvignon
Alcohol 14%
Importer Gilbeys
Stockists Kellys, Artane · McHughs, Kilbarrack · Jus de Vine, Portmarnock · Greenacres, Wexford · Lonergans, Clonmel · Vineyard, Galway +

Price £10-£11 (€12.70-€13.95)

**Casa Lapostolle Cuvée Alexandre Merlot
Rapel 1998**

Made from 50-year-old vines and aged in French oak under the eye of leading Bordeaux wine consultant Michel Rolland (Le Pin, Angélus etc, see also Château Méaume page 129), this is a Chilean to be taken seriously. Sweet, intense, plummy fruit is held in check by a firm structure, so there's all the harmony and length you'd hope for.

Grape Merlot
Alcohol 13.5%
Importer Comans
Stockists Redmonds, Ranelagh · Cooneys, Harold's Cross · McHughs, Kilbarrack · Londis, Malahide · Jus de Vine, Portmarnock · Ryan Vine, Navan +

Price about £16 (€20.30)

Edgewood Estate Napa Valley Cabernet Sauvignon 1996

Next time you're wondering what to serve at a dinner party (see page 253), consider this polished performer. While some Californian Cabernets are a tad too lush (and/or too expensive), this elegant wine counters its ripe blackcurrant character with enough mint-sprigged acidity and supple tannin to make it really attractive. It's just right for drinking now - and the tall bottle is handsome, too.

Grape Cabernet Sauvignon, Merlot
Alcohol 13.5%
Importer Dunnes Stores
Stockists Dunnes Stores leading outlets

Price about £13.50 (€17)

**Bonterra Cabernet Sauvignon, North Coast
Fetzer 1998**

Although all of Fetzer's output may be organic in a few years'
time, only the Bonterra range goes the full distance so far. I'm
a fan; to me these wines have layered, vibrant flavours and good
concentration. The Cabernet, rich and tempting with its
damsony fruit, herbal notes and peppery length, is my favourite.
(The Chardonnay is also recommended - see page 74.)

Grapes Cabernet Sauvignon, Syrah
Alcohol 13%
Importer Edward Dillon
Stockists Tesco · Molloys · Raheny Wine Cellar · Lord Mayor's,
Swords · Lawlors, Carlow · Wine Centre, Kilkenny ++

Price £13-£14 (€16.50-€17.80)

NORTH AMERICA

Ravenswood Vintners Blend Zinfandel
California 1998

This may be the entry-level wine from the team of Zinfandel freaks at Ravenswood, Sonoma's funkiest winery, but it's terrific. Luxurious dark fruits cloak punchy flavours of herbs and cracked pepper - making for a vigorous wine that is juicy enough to hold its charm. A winner with rich and spicy fusion dishes.

Grape Zinfandel
Alcohol 13.5%
Importer Woodford Bourne
Stockists Mitchells, Kildare St & Glasthule · Martha's Vineyard, Rathfarnham · Jus de Vine, Portmarnock · Cheers-Gibneys, Malahide ·Vineyard, Galway · Macs, Limerick +

Price about £14 (€17.80)

Sebastiani Sonoma County Old Vines Zinfandel 1998

Made from the intensely flavoured fruit of 50-to-100-year-old vines in Dry Creek Valley and Sonoma, this is an exuberant example of California's speciality grape, Zinfandel - berry-rich, peppery and bold. Somehow you don't expect a vast commercial enterprise like Sebastiani to come up with so much flavour and personality.

Grape Zinfandel
Alcohol 14%
Importer Barry & Fitzwilliam
Stockists selected Superquinns · Vaughan Johnsons, Temple Bar · Kielys, Mount Merrion · DeVine Wine Shop, Castleknock · Hennessys, Blessington · Scallys, Blackrock, Cork +

Price about £14 (€17.80)

NORTH AMERICA

Domaine Drouhin Oregon Pinot Noir
1996

Together, the Burgundian wine-making skills of Véronique Drouhin and the climate of the Pacific Northwest create what for me ranks as the New World's most exquisite Pinot Noir. Like good Burgundy, it has an ethereal quality which can't be captured in a few glib phrases, but there's also wonderful suppleness and a sense of immediate pleasure - attributes that sometimes elude its French counterparts. I could drink this till I die.

Grape Pinot Noir
Alcohol 13.5%
Importer Gilbeys
Stockists Sweeneys, Dorset St · McCabes, Blackrock & Foxrock · Deveneys, Dundrum · Jus de Vine, Portmarnock · Greenacres, Wexford · Vineyard, Galway +

Price about £27 (€34.30)

Domaine Drouhin
OREGON

PINOT NOIR
PRODUCED, BOTTLED BY DOMAINE DROUHIN OREGON · DUNDEE, OR 97115
IMPORTÉ PAR J. DROUHIN A F-21200 FRANCE
VIN DE L'ETAT D OREGON, USA
13.0% vol   750 ml

Clos Malverne Basket Pressed Pinotage Reserve Stellenbosch 1999

I'm not easily won over by Pinotage, but this modern example is seriously seductive. (If you doubt my word, pay heed to *Wine Spectator* which gave this 1999 the highest rating among a dozen of South Africa's big guns.) Pinotage fanatic Seymour Pritchard uses a mix of old and new techniques (open fermenters, basket presses, much riper grapes than before) to achieve voluptuous brambly fruit, luxurious texture, spicy oomph and subtle earthiness. Oh, and value too.

Grape Pinotage
Alcohol 13.5%
Importer Dunnes Stores
Stockists Dunnes Stores leading outlets

Price about £9 (€11.45)

Jordan Chameleon Cabernet Sauvignon-Merlot Stellenbosch 1998

Some of South Africa's smartest wines are coming from the impeccable estate of California-trained Gary and Kathy Jordan. This classic red blend marries distinctly Bordeaux-like aromas with the sweet cassis flavours and soft tannins of sun-ripened Cape fruit. Although high in alcohol, it comes across as suave. To be found in more restaurants than shops.

Grapes Cabernet Sauvignon, Merlot, Cabernet Franc
Alcohol 14%
Importer Maxxium
Stockists selected O'Briens outlets · Carvills, Camden St · Pottery Vine, Cabinteely · DeVine Wines, Letterkenny +

Price about £13 (€16.50)

Rust en Vrede Cabernet Sauvignon
Stellenbosch 1997

Harmony, poise, delicacy . . . those are some of the key words
you could apply to this outstanding Cabernet which combines
ripe, South African fruit and the mineral elements that charac-
terise the country's reds with a lingering savoury appeal that
seems more European. Produced only in limited quantities -
and it has that hand-crafted feel.

Grape Cabernet Sauvignon
Alcohol 13%
Importer O'Briens
Stockist O'Briens

Price about £14 (€17.80)

SOUTH AFRICA

Hamilton Russell Vineyards Pinot Noir
Walker Bay 1999

Anthony Hamilton Russell's wines - Chardonnay (see page 79) and Pinot Noir - are as civilised and elegant as the man himself. Still young and taut, with smouldering oak and earthy intrigue melding into concentrated cherry fruit, this gloriously complex Pinot would be well worth keeping for a year or two. A true South African classic.

Grape Pinot Noir
Alcohol 13.5%
Importer Gilbeys
Stockists Vintry, Rathgar · Raheny Wine Cellar · McHugh's, Kilbarrack · Mill Wine Cellar, Maynooth · Vineyard, Galway · Greenacres, Wexford ++

Price £18-£19 (€22.90-€24)

**Jacob's Creek Chardonnay-Pinot Noir
Orlando NV**

Wine snobs may turn their noses up at the mere mention of Jacob's Creek but, as is the case with some of the still wines under the JC label, this effort isn't half bad. Among the less expensive Aussie sparkling wines, it stands out as one of the most quaffable. A nice, gentle fizz with plenty of easy fruit, it's a touch drier (and cheaper) than rival Californians. Frivolous and fun.

Grapes Chardonnay, Pinot Noir
Alcohol 12%
Importer Irish Distillers
Stockists widely available

Price £10-£11 (€12.70-€13.95)

AUSTRALIA

Jansz Premium Non Vintage Brut Cuvée
Tasmania

From the cool Tasmanian outpost of major Australian player;
Yalumba, this relative newcomer to Ireland is the sort of
sparkling wine that can slip down at head-spinning speed. It's
light and crisp, with delicate, slightly honeyed fruit and a long,
firm finish. Not hugely complex - more of a charming crowd-
pleaser.

Grapes Chardonnay, Pinot Noir, Pinot Meunier
Alcohol 12.5%
Importer Cassidy · Oddbins
Stockists Teggarts, Rathgar · Berry Bros, Harry St ·
Bennetts, Howth · Cheers-Wicklow Arms, Delgany ·
Ardkeen, Waterford · O'Donovans, Cork · Oddbins +

Price £15-£16 (€19-€20.35)

Green Point by Chandon Brut
Yarra Valley 1997

I'd much rather drink this finely tuned sparkler from Möet's Australian operation than the champagne from its French base - and save up to a tenner into the bargain. (The price band, you'll notice, is extremely wide.) After the unusually fat and ripe 1996, 1997 sees Green Point back on form, with lovely aromas of baked apples and shortbread, and lingering firmness on the palate as well as ample fruit.

Grapes Pinot Noir, Chardonnay
Alcohol 12.5%
Importers Fèbvre · Oddbins
Stockists Vintry, Rathgar · Redmonds, Ranelagh · McCabes, Blackrock · Kellys, Clontarf · O'Keeffes, Kilcock · Oddbins ++

Price £16-£22 (€20.32-€27.95)

SOUTH

FRANCE

Domaine de l'Aigle Tradition Brut, Limoux
Jean-Louis Denois NV

There's nothing wishy-washy about this sparkler from Limoux in the south of France. Made from the classic champagne grapes by the champagne method, barrel-fermented for extra richness, it has ripe pear-and-apple flavours augmented by the yeasty, creamy character of fairly serious fizz - ending in a long, firm finish. A big, bold mouthful.

Grapes Pinot Noir, Chardonnay
Alcohol 12%
Importer River Wines
Stockist River Wines

Price about £12 (€15.25)

Deutz Marlborough Cuvée
Brut NV

A joint effort from champagne house Deutz and NZ colossus Montana, this stylish New Zealander scores top marks for bracing freshness and refinement at a reasonable price. While slightly softer sparkling wines seem to go down best at morning drinks parties, this crisp, invigorating fizz makes a terrific pre-dinner aperitif.

Grapes Chardonnay, Pinot Noir
Alcohol 12%
Importer Oddbins
Stockist Oddbins

Price about £14 (€17.80)

NEW ZEALAND

Deutz Blanc de Blanc Marlborough Cuvée 1996

Here you have the supremely elegant older sister of Deutz Marlborough Cuvée NV, recommended on the previous page. Made entirely from Chardonnay, this vintage sparkler is light-footed, with zesty top notes but underlying power and persistence of flavour. Classy, but is it worth the extra few pounds? Try them both and see!

Grape Chardonnay
Alcohol 12%
Importer Oddbins
Stockist Oddbins

Price about £17 (€21.60)

Pelorus Brut
Cloudy Bay 1996

I have the same relationship with Pelorus, the sparkling wine of New Zealand's famous winery Cloudy Bay, as with an extremely extrovert friend. Sometimes delight at our re-acquaintance, sometimes a touch of weariness. The style is unapologetic - ripe, toasty, yeasty, rich. There's quite a bit of vintage variation: Pelorus from the hot year of 1996 is, dare I say it, a tad blousy - but this is serious fizz, and the bottle scoops the top beauty prize.

Grapes Pinot Noir, Chardonnay
Alcohol 13%
Importer Findlater
Stockists selected Superquinns · Mitchells, Kildare St & Glasthule · Bourkes, Cabinteely · Noble Rot, Navan · Old Stand, Mullingar · O'Donovans, Cork ++

Price about £22 (€27.95)

Graham Beck Brut
Robertson NV

Made by the champagne method - or, as we're in South Africa, the method known as *Cap classique* - this is a soft, easy-going sparkler at a pretty good price. Ripely fruity (you'll sniff dessert apples, peaches and a lick of honey), it opens out into a broad, creamy finish with just a hint of toastiness. Bliss with strawberry shortcake!

Grapes Chardonnay, Pinot Noir
Alcohol 11.5%
Importer Cassidy
Stockists Bourkes, Cabinteely · McCabes, Blackrock & Foxrock · Londis, Maynooth · Bradys, Shankill · Scallys, Blackrock, Cork +

Price about £13 (€16.60)

Tesco Cava Brut
NV

Spanish Cava stands at the bargain end of the fizz market - or would if Ireland didn't levy punitive duty on every bottle of sparkling wine, from the most rubbishy to the most refined. There's a fair bit of nasty, rather vegetal Cava around, but this one is attractive - light and very refreshing with no sour notes.

Grapes Macabeo, Xarel-lo, Parellada, Chardonnay
Alcohol 11.5%
Importer Tesco
Stockist Tesco

Price about £9 (€11.45)

SPAIN

Segura Viudas Cava Brut Reserva NV

From the smaller sister company of the giant Freixenet, this is a slightly grander Cava with subtle, biscuity overtones, plenty of fruit and all the freshness you might long for on a summer's day. Smooth pear-and-sherbet flavours lead into a crisp, dry finish with respectable length. Very pleasant fizz indeed.

Grapes Macabeo, Parellada, Xarel-lo
Alcohol 11.5%
Importer Oddbins
Stockist Oddbins

Price about £10 (€12.70)

Champagne Pierre Gimonnet Cuis Premier Cru Blanc de Blancs Brut NV

Growers in Cuis since the 18th century, the Gimonnets have Chardonnay plantings in excellent sites – enabling them to make deliciously fruity but fine-boned champagnes like this light, bracing example with both power and vigour in the follow-through. What style on a champagne shoestring! Look out for their superb vintage Gastronome Brut, too.

Grape Chardonnay
Alcohol 12%
Importer Oddbins
Stockist Oddbins

Price about £18 (€22.85)

F R A N C E

FRANCE

**Champagne Billecart-Salmon
Brut Réserve NV**

Champagne aficionados would stab each other with cocktail sticks to reach a Billecart-Salmon bottle at a party. It's easy to understand why. From a small house with a big reputation, the zesty non-vintage dances across even the most jaded palate with wonderful, appley freshness leading into a long, creamy finish. Extremely refined.

Grapes Pinot Meunier, Chardonnay, Pinot Noir
Alcohol 12%
Importers James Nicholson, Oddbins
Stockists James Nicholson Direct · McCabes, Blackrock · DeVine Wine Shop, Castleknock · Noble Rot, Navan · Mill Wine Cellar, Maynooth · Oddbins +

Price £24–£26 (€30.50–€33)

Berrys' United Kingdom Cuvée
Brut NV

Berrys' own-label, non-vintage champagne, supplied by the small family-run house of Binet for the past 90 years, is an attractive, middle-of-the-road style. Plenty of soft, ripe fruit, plenty of freshness and creamy smoothness make for the sort of easy charm that empties glasses frighteningly fast.

Grapes Pinot Noir, Pinot Meunier, Chardonnay
Alcohol 12%
Importer Berry Bros
Stockist Berry Bros, Harry St

Price about £25 (€31.75)

CHAMPAGNE
SELECTED CUVÉE BY

Berry Bro. & *Rudd L*ᵗᵈ

BRUT

UKC

12% vol   75cl ℮

BINET FILS & Cᴵᴱ
PRODUCED BY N.M. 454-001 à 51461-F
MA-1154-05-00454

FRANCE

Champagne Joseph Perrier Cuvée Royale Brut NV

Not to be confused with Laurent-Perrier, the much smaller, less hyped house of Joseph Perrier makes a non-vintage champagne that stands out from the crowd. Tempting aromas of brioche and stewed apples lead into a vigorous attack on the palate, which soon settles into creamy breadth and an emphatically firm, dry finish.

Grapes Chardonnay, Pinot Noir, Pinot Meunier
Alcohol 12%
Importer Comans
Stockists Redmonds, Ranelagh · Martha's Vineyard, Rathfarnham · Martins, Fairview · Gerrys, Skerries · Ashford Food & Wine, Co. Wicklow · Mill Wine Cellar, Maynooth +

Price £26–£27 (€33–€34.30)

Champagne Charles Heidsieck
Brut Réserve NV, Mis en Cave 1997

Heidsieck's *mis en cave* range has managed to confound the wine trade, never mind consumers. (It's non-vintage: the year indicates the date of bottling and cellaring, not the harvest.) Do look out for it, all the same. This is a well-made champagne with generous fruit and a soft, creamy, vanilla cushion to give it broad appeal. Keep it another year or two and it will develop toasty richness.

Grapes Chardonnay, Pinot Noir, Pinot Meunier
Alcohol 12%
Importer Maxxium
Stockists Superquinn · Tesco · selected SuperValus · selected Centras · Roches Stores ++

Price £27-£28 (€34.30-€35.50)

FRANCE

Champagne Veuve Clicquot 'Yellow Label' Brut NV

One of Champagne's great mysteries is how Veuve Clicquot manages to keep the quality of the popular Yellow Label so consistently high when it is produced in such prodigious quantities. It's the NV that has everything - good fruit, good acidity, good length and above all, subtlety - all in one smooth, elegant mouthful. Easy to find, hard to beat.

Grapes Pinot Noir, Chardonnay, Pinot Meunier
Alcohol 12%
Importer Findlater
Stockists widely available

Price £28-£29 (€35.50-€36.85)

Champagne Pol Roger 'White Foil'
Brut NV

Winston Churchill's beloved champagne is one of my absolute favourites, too. Freshness, power and finesse are its hallmarks; quality and consistency remain long-term attributes of the modestly sized, family-run house of Pol Roger. Few champagnes wake up the palate (or raise drooping eyelids) in quite such an invigorating way.

Grapes Chardonnay, Pinot Noir, Pinot Meunier
Alcohol 12%
Importers Barry & Fitzwilliam · Oddbins
Stockists selected Superquinns · Roches Stores · Layden Wines, Liffey St · Redmonds, Ranelagh · selected Cheers Take-Home outlets · Oddbins +

Price £29-£30 (€36.85-€38)

FRANCE

Champagne Louis Roederer
Brut Premier NV

Roederer Cristal has hogged the limelight to such a degree that it's sometimes forgotten this house makes top quality non-vintage champagne too. Green-apple-crisp and fresh when just released, it soon develops creamy, biscuity tones with a hint of vanilla coming from Roederer's wood-aged reserve wines. Very stylish indeed.

Grapes Pinot Noir, Pinot Meunier, Chardonnay
Alcohol 12%
Importer J & T Davy
Stockists Searsons, Monkstown · Mitchells, Kildare St & Glasthule · Redmonds, Ranelagh · Cheers-Gibneys, Malahide · Wicklow Wine Co. ++

Price about £30 (€38)

FRANCE

Champagne Bollinger Special Cuvée
Brut NV

Full-bodied and firm with a reverberating, toasty aftertaste, Bollinger is so distinctive that you're unlikely ever to confuse it with any other champagne. Because it's quite weighty - rich yet almost austere at the same time - some people find it difficult to knock back in quantity. I must say I've never had that problem! One of the greats - but it's better with food (even the merest nibble) than alone.

Grapes Pinot Noir, Chardonnay, Pinot Meunier
Alcohol 12%
Importer Woodford Bourne
Stockists many good wine merchants

Price about £35 (€44.50)

SPAIN

Tesco Fino

Made by the bodega of José Estevez, the sand-for-bottle-manufacture millionaire who took over the old sherry house of Real Tesoro, this hasn't quite as much bite and zest as some finos, but boy is it pleasant all the same. Light and smoothly almondy, it has surprisingly persistent flavours considering the bargain price.

Grape Palomino
Alcohol 15%
Importer Tesco
Stockist Tesco

Price full bottle about £7 (€8.90)

SPAIN

Manzanilla La Gitana
Hidalgo

The old family firm of Hidalgo in Sanlucar de Barrameda, the salty coastal home of manzanilla, makes superb sherries at wonderfully affordable prices. This one glides from bracing, iodine freshness into delicate nutty tones that are amplified in a firm and majestic finish. A sherry aristocrat.

Grape Palomino
Alcohol 15%
Importer James Nicholson
Stockists James Nicholson Direct · Cheers-Gibneys, Malahide · Redmonds, Ranelagh · Ryan Vine, Navan · Le Caveau, Kilkenny

Price full bottle about £10 (€12.70)

SPAIN

Fino Inocente
Valdespino

The only single vineyard fino sherry made today is a special treat. From the famous and fiercely traditional bodega of A. R. Valdespino, this has all the freshness, subtlety and lingering, nutty complexity that make good dry sherry such a brilliantly invigorating drink.

Grape Palomino
Alcohol 16.5%
Importer J & T Davy
Stockists Searsons, Monkstown · Redmonds, Ranelagh · McCabes, Blackrock & Foxrock · Vintry, Rathgar · DeVine Wine Shop, Castleknock · DeVine Wines, Letterkenny +

Price half bottle about £6 (€7.60)
full bottle about £11 (€13.95)

Emilio Lustau Solera Reserva
Manzanilla Papirusa

It's positively heartwarming to see half-bottles from the out-standing Lustau range of sherries creeping into more and more shops. Long-established and fastidious, Lustau is a connoisseur's delight. While I also love their Puerto Fino and Jaraña Fino, this exquisitely refined, delicately salty manzanilla is an out-and-out favourite.

Grape Palomino
Alcohol 15.5%
Importer Woodford Bourne
Stockists Mitchells, Kildare St & Glasthule · selected Superquinns · selected SuperValus and many independent off-licences

Price half bottle £7-£8 (€8.90-€10)
           full bottle £11-£12 (€13.95-€15.25)

13 SWEET WINES -
With Dessert or as Dessert

AUSTRALIA

Penfolds Magill Tawny
Barossa Valley NV

From the Barossa - Australian home of port-style wines for over a century - comes this well-made, toasty-rich tawny. Aromas of toffee apples and caramelised oranges herald initial sweetness on the palate, but it's balanced by good acidity and lovely, nutty length. Nuts, in fact, are the very thing to enjoy with this.

Grapes Grenache, Shiraz
Alcohol 19%
Importer Findlater
Stockists Raheny Wine Cellar · Vintry, Rathgar · SuperValu, Wexford · Wine Centre, Kilkenny · Egans, Drogheda · Fahys, Ballina ++

Price half bottle about £8 (€10)

D'Arenberg The Noble Riesling
McLaren Vale 1997/1998

D'Arenberg's fourth-generation family winemaker, Chester Osborn, likes nothing better than experimentation. Launched in 1985, his botrytis Riesling is now an Aussie classic. Like a good marmalade, it combines intense sweetness with a refreshing and prolonged citrussy tang. Try it after a few years and the flavours will have moved towards raisins, dates and figs.

Grape Riesling
Alcohol 12.5%
Importers Taserra · Oddbins
Stockists McCabes, Blackrock & Foxrock · Carvills, Camden St · McHughs, Kilbarrack · Old Stand, Mullingar · Al Vino's, Athlone · Shannon Knights, Shannon · Oddbins +

Price half bottle £14–£15.50 (€17.80–€19.70)

FRANCE

Mitchell's Gold, Graves Supérieures
1997

Although Sauternes, the great sweet wine of Bordeaux, can be sublime, it tends to come at a rather scarifying price. Here's an affordable alternative. Enticing aromas of oranges and honey pave the way for a light, fruity, balanced dessert wine that is neither cloying nor too alcoholic. It may not be complex but there are intriguing hints of botrytis, the so-called 'noble rot' that great sweet wines depend on.

Grapes Sauvignon Blanc, Semillon
Alcohol 12.5%
Importer Mitchell & Son
Stockist Mitchells, Kildare St & Glasthule

Price about £10 (€12.70)

FRANCE

Muscat de Beaumes de Venise
Domaine de Durban 2000

After a period of wild popularity in the 1980s, the southern-Rhône dessert wine Beaumes de Venise has fallen out of favour - and not much wonder, because the examples seen here most frequently are horrifically, heavily sweet. Durban is different: much lighter, much more citrussy - much, much more delicious. Give it a chance.

Grape Muscat Blanc à Petits Grains
Alcohol 15%
Importer Barry & Fitzwilliam
Stockists selected Superquinns · Mortons, Ranelagh · Terroirs, Donnybrook · McCabes, Blackrock & Foxrock · Country Choice, Nenagh · Greenacres, Wexford +

Price **half bottle £9-£9.50 (€11.45-€12.35)**
         full bottle £15-£16 (€19-€20.35)

Banyuls Rimage
Domaine du Mas Blanc 1997

Here's something worth remembering: Banyuls, the extraordinary sweet red of Roussillon, is one of the few wines that goes brilliantly with chocolate. And this, from leading producers Dr Parcé et Fils, is one of the very best. Gorgeous flavours of macerated black fruits and dates lead into a long, smooth, mocha-edged finish.

Grape Grenache
Alcohol 17%
Importer Wines Direct
Stockist Wines Direct

Price under £19 (about €24)

**Berrys' Own Selection Sauternes
NV**

True fans will happily fork out anything from £50 to £500 for a venerable first-growth Sauternes like Yquem, Rieussec or Suduiraut. The rest of us sometimes just crave a wine with echoes of that greatness - the citrussy intensity, the dazzling acidity, the strange whiff of 'noble rot', all without sugar over-load. This one does the trick for what counts, in Sauternes terms, as a modest outlay.

Grapes Semillon, Sauvignon Blanc
Alcohol 13%
Importer Berry Bros
Stockist Berry Bros, Harry St

Price 50cl bottle about £17 (€21.60)

Tokaji Aszú 5 Puttonyos (Biue Label)
Royal Tokaji Wine Company 1995

The famous Hungarian sweet wine Tokaji, adored by Louis XIV
and the Russian tsars, is one of the great classics of the wine
world - a treat not to be missed. With fabulously concentrated flavours of honey, apricots and candied peel, it marries
intense sweetness with tongue-tingling, citrussy acidity. Splendid
with foie gras, blue cheese or on its own … and they say it's
liquid Viagra!

Grapes Harslevelu, Furmint
Alcohol 11%
Importer Findlater
Stockists O'Briens · McCabes, Blackrock & Foxrock · Kellys,
Clontarf · McCambridges, Galway · Fahys, Ballina +

Price 50cl bottle £22-£23 (€27.95-€29)

10 Terrific Aperitifs

10 Dinner Party Classics

White

Red

Sweet

10 Smart Dinner Choices

White

Red

Sweet

10 Great Wines for Casual Entertaining

White

Red

10 Party Crackers

10 Organic Wines

White

Red

10 Big Brands that won't Let You Down

Directory of Wine Stockists

Al Vinos
Irishtown, Athlone · tel (0902) 74589

Ardkeen Quality Foodstore
The Dunmore Road, Waterford · tel (051) 874620

Ashford Food & Wines
Ballanahinch Road, Ashford, Co. Wicklow · tel (0404) 40033

Bennetts of Howth
1a Laurence Road, Howth, Co. Dublin · tel/fax (01) 8325021

Berry Bros
4 Harry Street, Dublin 2 · tel (01) 6773444

Blessings
92 Main Street, Cavan · tel (049) 4331138

Bourkes Fine Wines
33a Johnstown Road, Dublin 18 · tel (01) 2850026

Brackens
191 Botanic Road, Glasnevin, Dublin 9 · tel (01) 8373467

Bradleys Supermarket and Off-Licence
81–82 North Main Street, Cork · tel (021) 4270845

Bradys of Shankill
Shangana Lounge, Shankill · tel (01) 2720500

Bubble Brothers
116a Lower Georges Street, Dún Laoghaire, Co. Dublin · tel (01) 2304117
English Market, Grand Parade, Cork · tel (021) 4254641

Burgundy Direct
8 Monaloe Way, Blackrock, Co. Dublin · tel (01) 2896615/2886239

Cana Wines
10 Castle Street, Mullingar, Co. Westmeath · tel (044) 42742

Carvills Off-Licence
39 Lower Camden Street, Dublin 2 · tel (01) 4751791

Centra
Head Office, Laurel House, Robinhood Industrial Estate, Dublin 22 ·
tel (01) 4194444
See also Musgraves in Directory of Importers

Cheers Take-Home
Head Office, Anglesea House, Anglesea Road, Ballsbridge, Dublin 4 ·
tel (01) 6680215
Baily Courts, Howth · tel (01) 8322691
Bradys, Shankill · tel (01) 2820153

Burnaby, Greystones · tel (01) 2874015
Comet, Santry · tel (01) 8427771
Gibneys, Malahide · tel (01) 8450606
Wicklow Arms, Delgany · tel (01) 2871616

Claudio's Wines
29 Drury Street, Dublin 2 · tel (01) 6715917

Connemara Hamper
Market Street, Clifden, Co. Galway · tel (095) 21054

Cooneys
197 Harolds Cross Road, Dublin 6W · tel (01) 4971671

Samuel C Copes
Castledermot, Athy, Co. Kildare · tel (0503) 44113

Costcutter
129 Ballymun Road, Dublin 9 · tel (01) 8378792

Country Choice
25 Kenyon Street, Nenagh, Co. Tipperary · tel (067) 32596

Cuisine de Vendange
1 Fallons Road, Naas, Co. Kildare · tel (045) 881793

C & T Supermarkets
Holmpatrick Estate, Shenick, Skerries · tel (01) 8492727

Dalys
Bridge Street, Boyle · tel (079) 62085

Deveneys Off-Licence Group
294 Harolds Cross Road, Dublin 6W · tel (01) 4923097
13 Main Street, Dundrum, Dublin 16 · tel (01) 2984288
1a Taney Road, Goatstown, Dublin 14 · tel (01) 2951745
16 Rathmines Road Upper, Dublin 6 · tel (01) 4972392
Sandyford SC, Sandyford, Dublin 18 · tel (01) 2957237
382 South Circular Road, Dublin 8 · tel (01) 4534932 · fax (01) 4926418

DeVine Wines
Pearse Road, Letterkenny, Co. Donegal · tel/fax (074) 20444

DeVine Wine Shop
Main Street, Castleknock, Dublin 15 · tel (01) 8209027

Drinkstore
87 Manor Street, Dublin 7 · tel (01) 6719760

Dunne & Crescenzi
14 South Frederick Street, Dublin 2 · tel (01) 6773815

Dunnes Stores
St Stephen's Green Shopping Centre, Dublin 2 · tel (01) 4780188
Ilac Centre, Dublin 1 · tel (01) 8730211
Branches nationwide

Duffys
92 Terenure Road East, Dublin 6 (01) 4905112

Egans
Main Street, Liscannor · tel (065) 7081430

Egan's Food Hall
Peter Street, Drogheda, Co. Louth · tel (041) 31810

Fahy's Supermarket
Garden Street, Ballina, Co. Mayo · tel (096) 22143

Feeneys
148 Lower Salthill, Galway · tel (091) 527881

Fields
Main Street, Skibbereen, Co. Cork · tel (028) 21400

Fine Wines Limerick
48 Roches Street, Limerick, Co. Limerick · tel (061) 417784
Jet Station, Ambassador Centre, Dooradoyle, Limerick ·
tel (061) 417276
Cosgraves Maxol Garage, Castletroy, Limerick · tel (061) 416501
Vintage House, 48 Roches Street, Limerick · tel (061) 416501

Foxs
119 Grafton Street, Dublin 2 · tel (01) 6770533

Galvins
Washington Street, Cork · tel (021) 4276314
Bandon Road, Cork · tel (021) 4316098
Douglas Road, Cork · tel (021) 4291100
Watercourse Road, Cork · tel (021) 500818

Gerry's Supermarket
31 Strand Street, Skerries, Co. Dublin · tel (01) 8490404

Good Food Store
Pembroke Lane, Ballsbridge · tel (01) 6675656

Gourmet Gallery
306 Rathmines Road, Rathmines, Dublin 6 · tel (01) 4977101

Greenacres
56 North Main Street, Wexford · tel (053) 22975

Hartes (Spar Supermarket)
By-pass Road, Clonakilty, Co. Cork · tel (023) 33116

Hennessys Off-Licence
Blessington, Co. Wicklow · tel (045) 865136

Higgins of Clonskeagh
34 Gledswood Drive, Dublin 14 · tel (01) 2697276

Il Primo Restaurant
16 Montague Street, Dublin 2 · tel (01) 4783373

irelandonwine.com
Naas Industrial Estate, Naas, Co. Kildare · tel (045) 899300

James Nicholson Direct
tel · (1890) 667799 · website www.jnwine.com

Joyce's of Knocknacarra
Shangort Road, Knocknacarra, Co. Galway · tel (091) 589300

Jus de Vine
Unit 10 Portmarnock Town Centre, Portmarnock, Co. Dublin
tel (01) 8461192

Karwig Wines
Kilnageary, Carrigaline, Co. Cork · tel (021) 4372864

Kelly's Wine Shop
27 Malahide Road, Artane, Dublin 5 · tel (01) 8311867

Kelly's Wine Vault
4 Vernon Ave, Clontarf, Dublin 3 · tel (01) 8335277

Kiely's
Mount Merrion, Co. Dublin · tel (01) 2832209

Kitchen Food Hall
Portlaoise, Co. Laois · tel (0502) 62061

Lawlors
The Harp Bar, Rathbilly, Carlow, Co. Carlow · tel (0503) 61112

Layden Fine Wines
14 Liffey Street, Dublin 1 · tel (01) 8377144

Le Caveau
The Market Yard, Kilkenny · tel (056) 52166

Listons
25 Lower Camden Street, Dublin 2 · tel (01) 4054779

Londis
Head Office, 160a Crumlin Road, Dublin 12 · tel (01) 4540688
Bridge Street, Carrick-on-Shannon, Co. Leitrim · tel (078) 21547
Yellow Walls Road, Malahide, Co. Dublin · tel (01) 8451511

Lonergans
O'Connell Street, Clonmel · tel (052) 21250

Lord Mayor's Off-Licence
Dublin Road, Swords, Co. Dublin · tel (01) 8409662

Loughnane's Food Hall
Main Street, Loughrea, Co. Galway · tel (091) 841229

Lynchs
Glanmire, Co. Cork · tel (021) 4822249

Mac's Off-Licence
Ennis Road, Limerick · tel (061) 453704

Magic Carpet
Cornelscourt, Co. Dublin · tel (01) 2895678

Marks & Spencer
24–29 Mary Street, Dublin 1 · tel (01) 8728833
15–20 Grafton Street, Dublin 1 · tel (01) 6797855
Liffey Valley, Dublin 22 · tel (01) 6161800
628 Patrick's Street, Cork · tel (021) 4275555

Martha's Vineyard
Rosemount Shopping Centre, Marion Road, Rathfarnham, Dublin 14 ·
tel (01) 4936918

Martins, Fairview
11 Marino Mart, Dublin 3 · tel (01) 8332952

McCabes Wines
51 Mount Merrion Ave, Blackrock, Co. Dublin ·
tel (01) 2882037
2 Brighton Road, Foxrock Village, Dublin 18 · tel (01) 2892689

McCambridge's
38 Shop Street, Galway · tel (091) 562259

McGrorys of Culdaff
Culdaff, Inishowen, Co. Donegal · tel (077) 79104

McHughs Off-Licence
57 Kilbarrack Road, Kilbarrack, Dublin 5 ·
tel/fax (01) 8394692

Michael's Wines
63 Deerpark Road, Mount Merrion, Dublin 14 ·
tel (01) 2780377

The Mill Wine Cellar
Mill Street, Maynooth · tel (01) 6291022/6291102

Mitchell & Son (Wine Merchants) Ltd
21 Kildare Street, Dublin 2 · tel (01) 6760766
54 Glasthule Road, Sandycove, Co. Dublin · tel (01) 2302301

Molloys Liquor Stores
Head Office, Block 2, Village Green, Tallaght, Dublin 24 ·
tel (01) 4515544 · fax (01) 4515658 · email molloys@indigo.ie
Ballyfermot, Dublin 10 · tel (01) 6262977
Ballymun, Dublin · tel (01) 8428189
Blanchardstown, Dublin 15 · tel (01) 8210129
Clondalkin, Dublin 22 · tel (01) 4570166
Clonsilla, Dublin 15 · tel (01) 8227144
Crumlin, Dublin 12 · tel (01) 4531611
Finglas, Dublin 11 · tel (010 8640251
Rathfarnham, Dublin · tel (01) 4936077
Santry, Dublin 9 · tel (01) 8622467
Village Green, Tallaght, Dublin 24 · tel (01) 4515544

Mortons
15 Dunville Avenue, Ranelagh, Dublin 6 · tel (01) 4971254

Mulqueens
36–41 Connolly Street, Nenagh · tel (067) 32611

Murtaghs
Enniskerry Village, Co. Wicklow · tel (01) 27604024

Next Door
Market Place, Cork · tel (021) 4304173
36 Thomas Davis Street, Cork ·
tel (021) 4398177

Noble Rot
48 Kennedy Road, Navan, Co. Meath · tel (046) 73489

O'Briens
Enquiries · tel 1850 269777
17 branches in Greater Dublin

O'Connors
Salthill House, Salthill, Co. Galway · tel (091) 523468

O'Donovan's Off-Licences
Shandon Street, Cork · tel (021) 4399121
Main Street, Cork · tel (021) 4613001
Oliver Plunkett Street, Cork · tel (021) 4277626
Bishopstown, Cork · tel (021) 4343416
Douglas East, Cork · tel (021) 4363650
Riversdale Shopping Centre, Midleton · tel (021) 4613792

O'Haras (SuperValu)
Main Street, Foxford · tel (094) 56409

O'Keeffes
Kilcock · (01) 6287225

Octavius Fine Wines
Grattan Street, Sligo · tel (071) 71730

Oddbins
17 Baggot Street Upper, Dublin 4 · tel (01) 6673033
360 Clontarf Road, Clontarf, Dublin 3 · tel (01) 8331653
125 Braemor Road, Churchtown, Dublin 14 · tel (01) 2963111
23 Rock Hill, Blackrock, Co. Dublin · tel (01) 2783844
Unit 6b, West End Retail Park, Blanchardstown, Dublin 15 ·
tel (01) 8243504

Old Stand
48 Dominic Street, Mullingar, Co. Westmeath · tel (044) 48910

On the Grapevine
21 St Patricks Road, Dalkey, Co. Dublin · tel (01) 2353054

Organico
2 Glengarriff Road, Bantry, Co. Cork · tel (027) 51391

The Pantry
O'Curry Street, Kenmare, Co. Kerry · tel (065) 9056576

Pettitts
Enniscorthy, Co. Wexford · tel (054) 34265
St Aidan's, Wexford · tel (053) 24055
Gorey · tel (055) 21722
Arklow · tel (0402) 39770
Athy · tel (0507) 38597

Pottery Vine
Dún Laoghaire, Co. Dublin · tel (01) 2847288

Quay Co-op
Sullivan's Quay, Cork · tel (021) 4317026

Raheny Wine Cellar (SuperValu)
Raheny Shopping Centre, Howth Road, Raheny, Dublin 5 · tel (01) 8310033

Redmonds of Ranelagh
25 Ranelagh Village, Dublin 6 · tel (01) 4971739/4960552

River Wines
Sandpit House, Termonfeckin, Co. Louth · tel (1850) 794637

Roches Stores
54 Henry Street, Dublin 1 · tel (01) 8730044
Branches nationwide
See also Musgraves in Directory of Importers

Ryan Vine
Trimgate Street, Navan, Co. Meath · tel (046) 78333

Scallys (SuperValu)
Skehard Road, Blackrock, Cork · tel (021) 4357388

Searsons Wine Merchants
The Crescent, Monkstown, Co. Dublin · tel (01) 2800405

Shannon Knights Inn
Town Centre, Shannon, Co. Clare · tel (061) 361045

Sky and Ground, Wexford
112 South Main Street, Wexford · tel (053) 21273

Superquinn
Head Office, Sutton Cross, Dublin 13 · tel (01) 8325700
Blackrock, Co. Dublin · tel (01) 2831511
Sutton, Dublin 13 · tel (01) 8322744
Branches nationwide

SuperValu
54 Henry Street, Dublin 1 · tel (01) 8730044
Branches nationwide
See also Musgraves in Directory of Importers

Sweeneys
20 Lower Dorset Street, Phibsborough, Dublin 7 ·
tel (01) 8749808
117 Philipburgh Avenue, Fairview, Dublin 3 · tel (01) 8372857

Teggarts Off-Licence
155 Rathgar Road, Dublin 6 · tel (01) 4977031

Terroirs
103 Morehampton Road, Donnybrook, Dublin 4 ·
tel (01) 6671311/66671146

Terrys
42 Roches Street, Limerick · tel (061) 412449

Tesco
Head Office, Gresham House, Marine Road, Dún Laoghaire,
Co. Dublin · tel (01) 2808441
Jervis Street, Dublin 1 · tel (01) 8780122
Branches nationwide

Thomas's
4 Brighton Road, Foxrock, Dublin 18 · tel (01) 2894101

Top Shop
Skerries Road, Lusk, Co. Dublin · tel (01) 8438335

Val Manning Emporium
Ballylickey, Bantry, Co. Cork · tel (027) 50456

Vaughan Johnson's Wine Shop
11a East Essex Street, Temple Bar, Dublin 2 · tel (01) 6715355

The Vineyard
14 Mainguard Street, Galway · tel/fax (091) 561816

The Vintry Off-Licence
102 Rathgar Road, Dublin 6 · tel (01) 4905477

Wicklow Wine Co.
Main St, Wicklow Town, Co. Wicklow · tel (0404) 66767

The Wine Bottle
Main Street, Dunshaughlin · tel (01) 8258135

Wine Centre
15 John Street, Kilkenny · tel (056) 21687

Wines Direct
Irishtown, Mullingar · tel (1800) 579579

Wine Vault
High Street, Waterford · tel (051) 853444

Wine Vault
68 Main Street, Portlaoise, Co. Laois · tel (0502) 62195

Wine World
Friary Street, Dungarvan, Co. Waterford · tel (058) 45600

Directory of Wine Importers

Allied Drinks
J F Kennedy Industrial Estate, Dublin 12 · tel (01) 4509777 ·
fax (01) 4509699 · email anne@allieddrinks.ie
Windsor Hill House, Glounthaune, Co. Cork · tel (021) 4353438 ·
fax (021) 4354362 · email info@allieddrinks.ie

Approach Trade Ireland
South Quay, Carrick-on-Suir, Co. Tipperary · tel (051) 640164 ·
fax (051) 641580 · mobile (087) 2332025

Barry & Fitzwilliam
Ballycurreen Industrial Estate, Airport Road, Cork · tel (021) 4320900 ·
fax (021) 4320910
50 Dartmouth Square, Dublin 6 · tel (01) 6671755/6606984 ·
fax (01) 6600479

Berry Bros
4 Harry Street, Dublin 2 · tel (01) 6773444 · email sales@bbr.ie

Bubble Brothers
43 Upper John Street, Cork · tel/fax (021) 4552252
116a Lower George's Street, Dún Laoghaire · tel (01) 2304117 ·
email info@bubblebrothers.com
website http://www.bubblebrothers.com

Burgundy Direct
8 Monaloe Way, Blackrock, Co. Dublin · tel (01) 2896615/2886239 ·
fax (01) 2898470 · email burgundy@indigo.ie

Cassidy Wines
1b Stillorgan Industrial Park, Stillorgan, Dublin 18 ·
tel (01) 2954157/4632 · fax (01) 2954477 · email info@cassidywines.iol.ie

Comans Wholesale
Belgard Road, Tallaght, Dublin 24 · tel (01) 4519146 ·
fax (01) 4519772 · email wine@comans.ie

Dunnes Stores
Head Office, 67 Upper Stephen Street, Dublin 8 · tel (01) 4751111 ·
fax (01) 4751441

Edward Dillon & Company
25 Mountjoy Square East, Dublin 1 · tel (01) 8193300 · fax (01) 8555852

Fèbvre & Co
15–17 Maple Avenue, Stillorgan Industrial Estate, Stillorgan, Co. Dublin ·
tel (01) 2959030 · fax (01) 2859036 · email febvre@eircom.net

Findlater Wine Merchants
Magna Drive, City West Business Campus, Dublin 24
tel (01) 4529112 · fax (01) 4529120 · email sales@findlaters.com

Gilbeys of Ireland
Nangor House, Nangor Road, Western Estate, Dublin 12
tel (01) 4194000 · fax (01) 4194001 (reception) · tel (01) 4194040
fax (01) 4194041 (sales) · email gilbeys.info@udv.com

Grants of Ireland
Kilcarberry Industrial Park, Nangor Road, Clondalkin, Dublin 22
tel (01) 6304100 · fax (01) 6304124 (customer service)
fax (01) 6304123 (other departments) · email grants@cantrell.ie

Hellenic Marketing
11 The Coppins, Castletown, Celbridge, Co. Kildare · tel (01) 6279201
fax (01) 6102283 · email dennisthompson@eircom.net

Irish Distillers Group
11–12 Bow St, Dublin 7 · tel (01) 8725566 · fax (01) 8723109
email info@idl.ie

irelandonwine.com
Naas Industrial Estate, Naas, Co. Kildare · tel (045) 899300
fax (045) 876656

J S Woods
6 Sandford Road, Ranelagh, Dublin 6 · tel (01) 4974041
fax (01) 4965299 · email radichio@eircom.net

J & T Davy
Monkstown Crescent, Blackrock, Co. Dublin · tel (01) 2800405
fax (01) 2804771

James Adams Vintners
1 Charleston Road, Ranelagh, Dublin 6 · tel (01) 4963866
fax (01) 4960186 · email adamsvintners@tinet.ie

James Nicholson
Unit 4, Santry Hall Industrial Estate, Dublin 9 · tel (1890) 667799
fax (048) 44830028 · email shop@jnwine.com
website www.jnwine.com

Karwig Wines
Kilnageary, Carrigaline, Co. Cork · tel (021) 4372864
fax (021) 4374159 · email info@karwig-wines.ie · website www.kar-
wig-wines.ie

Kelly & Co
Unit 5 Park West Industrial Estate, Nangor Road, Dublin 12 ·
tel (01) 8554366 · fax (01) 6234155 · email prenier@kellywines.com

Koala Wines
25 Seatown, Dundalk, Co. Louth · tel (048) 41752804 ·
fax (048) 41752943 · email koalawines@ireland1.fsbusiness.co.uk

MacCormaic Vintners
116a Terenure Road North, Dublin 6W · tel (01) 4907928 ·
fax (01) 4907930 · email maccormaicvintners@eircom.net

Mackenway Distributors
4 The Park Business Centre, Cabinteely, Dublin 18 · tel (01) 2848411 ·
email mackenway@eircom.net

Marks & Spencer
24–29 Mary Street, Dublin 1 · tel (01) 8728833

Mary Pawle Wines (importers/distributors of organic wine)
Gortamullen, Kenmare · tel (064) 41443 · mobile (087) 2265967 ·
email marypawlewines@ocean.free.net

Maxxium
Rembrandt House, 1 Longford Terrace, Monkstown, Co. Dublin ·
tel (01) 2804341 · fax (01) 2801805

Mitchell & Son
21 Kildare Street, Dublin 2 · tel (01) 6760766 · fax (01) 6611509 ·
email michkst@indigo.ie · website http://mitchellandson.com

Morgans Wine Merchants
20 Clanwilliam Square, Dublin 2 · tel (01) 6627752 ·
fax (01) 6627756 · email morgans@iol.ie

Musgraves
Head Office, Tramore Road, Cork · tel (021) 4803000
St Margaret's, Ballymun, Dublin 11 · tel (01) 8428472
Laurel House, PO Box 929, Robinhood Industrial Estate, Clondalkin,
Dublin 22 · tel (01) 4501442 · fax (01) 4505249 ·
email svcd@musgrave.ie · website http://www.musgrave.ie

O'Briens Wine Off-Licence Group
Unit 33, Spruce Avenue, Stillorgan Industrial Park, Co. Dublin ·
tel (01) 2693139 · fax (01) 2697480 ·
email accounts@obriensgroup.ie ·
website www.obrienswine.ie

Oddbins
17 Baggot Street, Dublin 2 · tel (01) 6673033 · fax (01) 6673109
website www.oddbins.com

Papillon Wines
55–56 North Strand Road, Dublin 3 · tel (01) 8561339 ·
mobile 087 2631922 · fax (01) 8554740 ·
email greg.grouse@oysterinfo.com

River Wines
Sandpit House, Termonfeckin, Co. Louth · tel (1850) 794637 ·
fax (041) 9822820 · email rvrwines@indigo.ie

Superquinn
PO Box 99, Sutton Cross, Dublin 13 · tel (01) 8325700/6302000

Taserra Wine Merchants
17 Rathfarnham Road, Terenure, Dublin 6W · tel (01) 4904047 ·
fax (010 4904052 · email wine@iol.ie

TDL Distributors
Naas Road, Clondalkin, Dublin 22 · tel (01) 4130100/4130150 ·
fax (01) 4130123 · email tdl@tdl.ie

Tesco
Head Office, Gresham House, Marine Road, Dún Laoghaire, Co. Dublin ·
tel (01) 2808441 · fax (01) 2800136

T P Reynolds
50–52 Pembroke Road, Ballsbridge, Dublin 4 · tel (01) 6600246 ·
email info@tpreynolds.com

Wines Direct
Lisamate, Irishtown, Mullingar, Co. Westmeath · tel (1800) 579579 ·
fax (044) 40015 · email winesdirect@wines-direct.com ·
website http://www.wines-direct.com

Woodford Bourne
79 Broomhill Road, Tallaght, Dublin 24 · tel (01) 4047300 ·
fax (01) 4599342 · email robt-roberts.ie

Wines Listed by Country

Wines Listed by Grape Variety

Agiorgitiko
Agiorgitiko Boutari, Nemea 104
Tsantali Nemea 103

Albariño
Martin Códax Albariño, Rías
    Baixas 31

Barbera
*Barbera, Nebbiolo, Cabernet
Sauvignon*
Airone Monferrato, Michele
    Chiarlo 164

Bonarda
Medrano Bonarda, Mendoza 117

Cabernet Franc
Marc Brédif Chinon 96
Saumur-Champigny Vieilles Vignes,
    Dom. Filliatreau 97

Cabernet Sauvignon
Casillero del Diablo Cabernet
    Sauvignon, Maipo, Concha y
    Toro 206
Castillo de Molina Cabernet
    Sauvignon Reserva, Lontue
    207
Cousino-Macul Antiguas Reservas
    Cabernet Sauvignon, Maipo
    209
D'Arenberg The Coppermine
    Road Cabernet Sauvignon,
    McLaren Vale 202
Enate Rosado Cabernet
    Sauvignon, Somontano 87
Geoff Merrill Cabernet Sauvignon
    Reserve, South Australia
    197
La Gavina Cabernet Sauvignon
    Toscana, Cecchi 162
Miguel Torres Santa Digna
    Cabernet Sauvignon Rosé,
    Curicó 80
Rust en Vrede Cabernet
    Sauvignon, Stellenbosch 219

Tesco Coonawarra Cabernet
    Sauvignon 188
Wakefield Cabernet Sauvignon,
    Clare Valley 185

*Cabernet Sauvignon, Cabernet
Franc*
Cabernet Roncaccio, Friuli,
    Collavini 109

*Cabernet Sauvignon, Carmen*ère
Santa Ines Cabernet Sauvignon,
    Maipo Valley 203

Cabernet Sauvignon, Merlot
Berrys' Own Selection Good
    Ordinary Claret NV 89
Edgewood Estate Napa Valley
    Cabernet Sauvignon 212
Greg Norman Estates
    Coonawarra Cabernet-Merlot
    198
Michel Lynch Bordeaux 128
Navarra Correas Colección
    Privada, Altos del Rio Mendoza
    183
Patache d'Aux Médoc Cru
    Bourgeois, Ch. 130

*Cabernet Sauvignon, Merlot,
Cabernet Franc*
de la Colline Bergerac, Ch.. 127
    Frank Phélan Saint-Estèphe
    132
Jordan Chameleon Cabernet
    Sauvignon-Merlot, Stellenbosch
    218

*Cabernet Sauvignon, Merlot,
Carmenère, Malbec*
Mont Gras Quatro Reserva,
    Colchagua 208

*Cabernet Sauvignon, Merlot,
Tempranillo*
Raimat Abadia, Costers del Segre
    173

Chardonnay, Verdelho
Brokenwood Harlequin
Unwooded Chardonnay-
Verdelho, South Eastern
Australia 69

Chardonnay, Viognier
de Montplaisir Chardonnay-
Viognier Cuvée Prestige, Vin de
Pays d'Oc, Dom. 62

Chenin Blanc
Blue White Chenin Blanc,
Stellenbosch, Old Vines 77
Gaudrelle Vouvray, Ch. 56
L'Avenir Chenin Blanc,
Stellenbosch 78
Marc Brédif Vouvray 57

Chenin Blanc, Sauvignon Blanc
Villiera Blue Ridge Blanc Chenin
Blanc-Sauvignon Blanc, Paarl 46

Corvina
Corvina, Molinara, Rondinella
Ripassa Valpolicella Classico
Superiore, Zenato 163
Zenato Amarone della Valpolicella
Classico, Veneto 167

Corvina, Rondinella, Molinara
Masi Campofiorin Ripasso, Rosso
del Veronese 160
Masi Valpolicella Classico
Superiore 107

Corvina, Rondinella, Molinara, Negrara
Villa Rizzardi Poiega Valpolicella
Classico Superiore 108

Furmint
Disnókö Dry Furmint, Tokaji 65

Gamay
Saint-Amour Les Bonnets,
J-B Patissier 90

Gewürztraminer
Trimbach Gewürztraminer,
Alsace 49

Grenache/Garnacha
Banyuls Rimage, Dom. du Mas
Blanc 248
Bergerie de l'Hortus Rosé de
Saignée, Pic Saint Loup 85
Gran Feudo Rosé, Navarra,
Bodegas Julian Chivite 86
Marques de Aragón Old Vine
Garnacha, Calatayud 172

Garnacha, Carinena
Torres Sangre de Toro, Catalunya
114

Garnacha, Carinena, Cabernet Sauvignon
Albet i Noya Lignum, Penedés
176
Les Terrasses, Priorat, Alvaro
Palacios 179

Garnacha, Tempranillo, Carinena, Cabernet Sauvignon
Mas Collet, Tarragona, Capçanes
174

Grenache, Shiraz
Penfolds Magill Tawny, Barossa
Valley NV 244

Grenache, Syrah
Guigal Côtes-du-Rhône 137

Grenache, Syrah, Cinsault, Mourvèdre
Belleruche Côtes-du-Rhône, M.
Chapoutier 99
La Vieille Ferme Côtes du
Ventoux 98

Grenache, Syrah, Mourvèdre
de Flaugergues Rosé Coteaux du
Languedoc La Méjanelle, Ch.
84

Mourvèdre, Grenache
Jean-Louis Denois Mourvèdre-
Grenache, Vin de Pays d'Oc
145

Mourvèdre, Syrah, Grenache
de Flaugergues, Coteaux du
Languedoc La Méjanelle, Ch.
150

Muscat Blanc á Petits Grains
Muscat de Beaumes de Venise,
Dom. de Durban 247

Negroamaro
Cappello di Prete Salento Rosso,
Candido 158

Nero D'Avola
Elorina Villa Dorato Eloro Rosso
157

Nero D'Avola, Perricone
Regaleali Rosso, Tasca d'Almerita
161

Palomino
Emilio Lustau Solera Reserva
Manzanilla Papirusa 243
Fino Inocente, Valdespino 242
Manzanilla La Gitana, Hidalgo 241
Tesco Fino 240

Periquita
J. P. Tinto Regional, Terras do Sado,
J. P. Vinhos 168
Periquita, Vinho Regional Terras
do Sado, J M da Fonseca 110

Pinotage
Clos Malverne Basket Pressed
Pinotage Reserve, Stellenbosch
217

Pinot Blanc
Berrys' Own Selection Alsace
Pinot Blanc 3

Hugel Alsace Pinot Blanc de
Blancs, Cuvée Les Amours 2

Pinot Gris/Pinot Grigio
Trimbach Alsace Pinot Gris
Réserve 48
Villa Canlungo Corno Rosazzo
Pinot Grigio, Friuli, Collavini
26

Pinot Meunier
*Pinot Meunier, Chardonnay, Pinot
Noir*
Champagne Billecart-Salmon
Brut Réserve NV 232

Pinot Noir
Aloxe-Corton, Dom. Latour
135
Bourgogne Hautes-Côtes de
Beaune, Pierre Ponnelle 92
Bourgogne Pinot Noir, Louis
Jadot 93
Bourgogne Vieilles Vignes, Dom.
Vincent Dancer 94
Coldstream Hills Pinot Noir, Yarra
Valley 195
Cono Sur Pinot Noir, Rapel 122
Drouhin Oregon Pinot Noir,
Dom 216
Givry Premier Cru Clos de la
Servoisine, Dom. Joblot 95
Hamilton Russell Vineyards Pinot
Noir, Walker Bay 220
Hunter's Pinot Noir, Marlborough
124
de Martinolles Pinot Noir, Vin de
Pays de l'Aude, Dom. 102
Mercurey Premier Cru Clos des
Myglands, Faiveley 134
Ninth Island Pinot Noir, Tasmania,
Piper's Brook 120
Piper's Brook Vineyard Estate
Pinot Noir, Tasmania 121
Savigny-les-Beaune Premier Cru
Les Lavières, Charles Viénot
133

Stoneleigh Vineyards
  Marlborough Sauvignon Blanc
  43
Vacheron Sancerre, Dom. 17
Villa Maria Reserve Wairau Valley
  Sauvignon Blanc, Marlborough
  73

Sauvignon Blanc, Semillon
Capel Vale Sauvignon Blanc-
  Semillon, Western Australia 37
Mitchell's Gold, Graves
  Supérieures 246
Owen's Estate Sauvignon Blanc-
  Semillon, South Eastern
  Australia, Geoff Merrill 32

Sauvignon Blanc, Semillon,
Muscadelle
Bertinerie Premières Côtes de
  Blaye, Ch 7
Pique-Sègue Montravel, Ch. 6

Semillon
Mount Pleasant Elizabeth Hunter
  Valley Semillon, McWilliams
  70
Peter Lehmann Barossa Semillon
  67

Semillon, Sauvignon Blanc
Berrys' Own Selection Sauternes
  NV 249
du Seuil Graves Sec, Ch. 52
Wolf Bass White Label Semillon-
  Sauvignon Blanc, South
  Australia 33

Syrah/Shiraz
Crozes-Hermitage, Dom. de
  Thalabert, Jaboulet Aîné 141
Fortant de France Syrah Rosé, Vin
  de Pays d'Oc 83
James Herrick Millia Passum
  Syrah, Vin de Pays d'Oc 148
Mount Pleasant Philip Hunter
  Valley Shiraz, McWilliams 119

Omrah Shiraz, Western Australia-
  McLaren Vale, Plantagenet 192
Peter Lehmann The Barossa
  Shiraz 187
Reynella Basket-Pressed Shiraz,
  McLaren Vale, Ch. 199
Rothbury Estate Brokenback
  Shiraz, Hunter Valley 194
de Sainte Marthe Syrah, Vin de
  Pays de Cassan, Dom. 144
St Hallett Old Block Shiraz,
  Barossa Valley 201
Tahbilk Shiraz, Victoria, Ch. 190
Tesco McLaren Vale Shiraz 186

Shiraz, Cabernet Sauvignon
Penfolds Koonunga Hill Shiraz-
  Cabernet Sauvignon, South
  Australia 189

Shiraz, Pinotage, Cabernet, Cinsout
Vaughan Johnson's Good Everyday
  Cape, Red, South Africa 126

Syrah, Grenache, Carignan
Maris Minervois, Comte Cathare,
  Ch. 143

Syrah, Grenache, Cinsault,
Mourvèdre
du Vieux Télégraphe
  Châteauneuf-du-Pape, Dom.
  142

Syrah, Mourvèdre, Grenache
Bergerie de l'Hortus Classique
  Pic Saint Loup 101

Tempranillo/Tinta del Pais/Tinta
Roriz
Condado de Haza, Ribera del
  Duero, Alejandro Fernandez
  178
Duas Quintas Douro,
  Ramos-Pinto 171
Gazur, Ribera del Duero, Telmo
  Rodriguez 175

Ochoa Tempranillo Crianza,
Navarra 112
Palacio de la Vega Tempranillo
Reserva, Navarra 177
Riscal Tempranillo, Castilla y Leon,
Marques de Riscal 115

*Tempranillo, Garnacha, Cabernet
Sauvignon*
Gran Feudo Crianza, Navarra,
Bodegas Julian Chivite 111

*Tempranilla, Garnacha, Cabernet
Sauvignon, Cariñena*
Can Vendrell Cabernet
Sauvignon-Tempranillo,
Penedès, Albet i Noya 113

Trebbiano
I Frati Lugana, Cà dei Frati 27
Lugana San Benedetto, Zenato 25

Vernaccia
Melini Le Grillaie Vernaccia di San
Gimignano 66

Viognier
Cono Sur Viognier, Rapel 72

*Viognier, Chardonnay, Sauvignon
Blanc*
Bergerie de l'Hortus Classique,
Vin de Pays du Val de
Montferrand 20

Zinfandel
Canepa Winemaker's Selection
Zinfandel, Curico 123
Ravenswood Vintners Blend
Zinfandel, California 214
Sebastiani Sonoma County Old
Vines Zinfandel 215

Other White Blends
Catarratto, Chardonnay
D'Istinto Catarratto-
Chardonnay, Sicilia 23

*Colombard, Gros Manseng,
Ugni Blanc*
du Rey, Vin de Pays des Côtes de
Gascogne, Dom. 5

*Garganega, Chardonnay, Trebbiano
di Soave*
San Vincenzo Soave Classico,
Anselmi 28

Harslevelu, Furmint
Tokaji Aszú 5 Puttonyos (Blue
Label), Royal Tokaji Wine
Company 250

Macabeo, Parellada, Xarel-lo
Segura Viudas Cava Brut Reserva
NV 230

Macabeo, Xarel-lo, **Parellada,
Chardonnay** Tesco Cava Brut
NV 229

Procanico, Grechetto, Verdello
Campogrande Orvieto Classico,
Antinori 24

Verdejo, Viura, Sauvignon Blanc
Con Class Selección Especial,
Rueda 29

Other Red Blends
*Periquita, Alfrocheiero, Trincadeira,
Aragonez, Moreto*
Tinto da Anfora, Vinho Regional
Alentejano, J.P. Vinhos 169

*Trincadeira, Aragonez, Tinta
Francesa*
D'Avillez, Vinho Regional
Alentejo, J M da Fonseca 170

Xinomavro, Stavroto, Krassato
Rapsani Reserve, Epilegmenos,
Tsantalis 152

Index of Wine Names